Scott O'Hara

Rarely Pure and Never Simple
Selected Essays of Scott O'Hara

Pre-publication
REVIEWS,
COMMENTARIES,
EVALUATIONS . . .

"**I**t is no surprise that Scott O'Hara took the title of this collection from one of Oscar Wilde's more famous epigrams. Like the great Oscar's witticisms, O'Hara's essays—as well as his mind and politics—are at once startling, perplexing, paradoxical, and sometimes (intentionally) irritating. From the aesthetics of tricking to lesbian porn, from unorthodox notions of "safe sex" to blithely anarchistic ideas about economics, Scott O'Hara is steadfast in his determination to speak his mind and provoke us into an immediate, forceful reaction. Like Wilde, O'Hara teases and taunts us into rethinking, re-imagining, and (yes, even sometimes) re-affirming our own ideas and politics. It is rare to find a writer willing—and able—to put himself on the line like this, and for this we owe him the respect of honest response."

Michael Bronski
Author, The Pleasure Principle: Sex, Backlash, and the Struggle for Gay Freedom

More pre-publication
REVIEWS, COMMENTARIES, EVALUATIONS . . .

"**S**cott O'Hara offered one of the most opinionated and unapologetic voices of the 1990s. Impulsive, vulnerable, revealing, painfully honest—O'Hara was never one to mince words. *Rarely Pure and Never Simple* offers an extensive collection of his numerous essays for gay presses and anthologies after the untimely demise of his highly influential *STEAM* magazine. This is perhaps his most unrestrained work published so far, freed from thematic constraints of autobiography, public sex, or pornography. O'Hara casts his keen eye across a wide spectrum of culture both gay and straight, offering his often brutal opinions on child-rearing, drugs, homelessness, performance art, theater, TV, politics, and, of course, sex.

From the pleasures of unprotected sex to the sublime flavor of persimmons, from skinheads to sushi, O'Hara's book offers an expansive portrait of his enthusiastic, big-hearted, and head-first embrace of life's joys. Even though there is something here to infuriate and offend most everyone—from his support of N.A.M.B.L.A. to what he liked about Colorado's Amendment 2—one cannot help but come away from this book feeling a shadow of O'Hara's sheer exuberance at being alive. His essays bring a flush to the cheeks, moisture to the palms, quickening to the pulse, blood to the groin, and electricity to the head. His vision, spirit, and sheer verve are as inspirational as they are audacious."

D. Travers Scott
Author, *Execution Texas: 1987*;
Editor, *Strategic Sex*

"**S**cott O'Hara had no use for dishonesty or cowardice. But perhaps he would have been surprised to know that he is one of the most honest and brave writers this culture has known. In an age of niceties, when the press release is the most dominant form of literature, *Rarely Pure and Never Simple* is refreshingly full of opinions, rants, revolutions, jeremiads, and incendiary beliefs. We find ourselves disagreeing, fighting, discrediting—but never ignoring—what O'Hara has to say. How then, do we find ourselves holding this book close to our hearts as something vitally important? Because if we are human, we love honesty and bravery."

Brian Bouldrey
Author,
San Francisco, CA

Rarely Pure and Never Simple
Selected Essays of Scott O'Hara

HAWORTH Gay & Lesbian Studies

John P. De Cecco, PhD
Editor in Chief

New, Recent, and Forthcoming Titles:

Rarely Pure
and Never Simple
Selected Essays of Scott O'Hara

Scott O'Hara

Harrington Park Press
An Imprint of The Haworth Press, Inc.
New York • London

Published by

Harrington Park Press, an imprint of The Haworth Press, Inc., 10 Alice Street, Binghamton, NY 13904-1580

The Haworth Press, Inc., 10 Alice Street, Binghamton, NY 13904-1580

Cover design by Monica Seifert.

Cover photo by Mark I. Chester.

The Library of Congress has cataloged the hardcover edition of this book as:

O'Hara, Scott.
    Rarely pure and never simple : selected essays of Scott O'Hara / Scott O'Hara.
        p.   cm.
    Includes bibliographical references.
    ISBN 0-7890-0573-5 (alk. paper).
    1. O'Hara, Scott. 2. Gay men—United States—Biography. 3. Gays—United States—Identity. I. Title.
HQ75.8.O53A3 1999
306.76′62—dc21   98-28104
                                                                                                         CIP

ISBN 1-56023-939-5 (pbk.)

CONTENTS

ABOUT THE AUTHOR

Scott "Spunk" O'Hara (1961-1998) was a well-known porn star who appeared in twenty-six films between 1983 and 1992. He was editor and publisher of the sex journal STEAM ("the literate queer's guide to sex and controversy") from 1993-1996 and was published in numerous anthologies, magazines, and newspapers. His first book of short stories, *Do-It-Yourself Piston Polishing (for Non-Mechanics),* was released in August 1996 by Badboy. His autobiography, *Autopornography: A Memoir of Life in the Lust Lane,* was published in 1997 by The Haworth Press, Inc. and was #14 on the "Books Bought Mainly by Men—1997 Top 100 Bestsellers" list as rated by A Different Light Bookstore. O'Hara died of AIDS-related complications in February of 1998.

Foreword

"His death was about as 'good' as a death can be: planned, ordered, with time for good-byes; not too much pain, no loss of mental faculties, very few of the 'indignities' that are associated with late-stage deaths. He was grateful for that. And the rest of us, well, we take comfort where we can find it."

So Scott O'Hara wrote me in a letter dated April 22, 1996, about the passing of a friend.

Scott was one of the last human beings alive who preferred writing letters to talking on the phone (or enduring the irritations of e-mail). One of his many change of address postcards is still tacked to my bulletin board. "Written words welcomed," it reads, "telephonic torture tolerated." "If I can go an entire twenty-four hours without hearing the phone ring," he writes in this book, "I consider that a successful day."

Dialing his number in early February 1998 I did not expect that he would answer. In fact, my dinner was ready. I was braced for another confrontation with his hostile answering machine: a militantly inhuman voice prompt and fifteen seconds in which to leave a message.

To my surprise, Scott picked up, and we talked for half an hour. He was anxious to hear my thoughts on the manuscript he'd sent me of *Rarely Pure and Never Simple*. Being taken off guard made it easier for me to be frank. I told him I'd relished his collection of sixty short essays and poems, but wondered whether it might not be just a little too long. I had been unable to get through it during a six-hour visit to a university tearoom woefully lacking in distractions (a tearoom, incidentally, that I had discovered through *STEAM*).

After howling with laughter, Scott agreed that this was indeed a bad sign, and offered to consider making some cuts. I assured him that the essays I had read were more enjoyable than what casual sex

I did have that day. Scott said that he knew just what I meant; his own lack of interest in what most people call sex was threatening to become a personal crisis. After all, what else would anyone want to hear about from the man who built his fame on having "The Biggest Dick in San Francisco"?

We didn't get around to discussing his health. When I mentioned that my dinner was getting cold, Scott said good night.

A week later, at 10:30 in the evening, I picked up the phone and someone said, "I'm here at San Francisco General Hospital with Scott O'Hara, who isn't expected to make it through the night. Scott would like to say good-bye. Here he is."

Talk about the impossibility of finding the right words. "I guess *you'll* have to make the cuts now, Steve," Scott laughed. "The book will sell better posthumously." I could not laugh, and after three or four minutes of at least managing not to say anything really stupid (I hope), I became a little choked up. At which point Scott excused himself.

He died twenty-four hours later, at home in San Francisco, surrounded by friends. He threatened that if they held a memorial ceremony he would come back and haunt them.

"Writer/publisher/performer Scott 'Spunk' O'Hara wishes to announce that he croaked at 10:40 p.m. on Wednesday, February 18," read the *Bay Area Reporter* obituary, which Scott wrote himself. "In lieu of flowers, he requests that you make a donation to your favorite sperm bank."

*   *   *

The boy who would legally change his name to Scott O'Hara was born in Grants Pass, Oregon, on October 16, 1961. The youngest of seven children, he grew up on a thirty-eight-acre farm a few miles outside of town. His parents—John Birchers and "puritanical" Presbyterians—may be said to have been slightly eccentric. His father was obsessed with flying saucers, and sometimes barbecued roadkill. Scott and his brothers did not sleep in their bedrooms, but outdoors on the lawn. Yet the family were not exactly "white trash." One day in his teen years a plank broke off a crate Scott had been using as a chair, revealing the contents: $50,000 in silver and gold.

It was then that he realized he would probably not have to worry about preparing for a typical career.

After high school Scott left home, traveling—by bicycle—to San Francisco, then all over the country. He put in a year at the University of Dallas. In Chicago, he married the lesbian ex-lover of his beloved sister Claudia, who had killed herself. Throughout the 1980s he relocated to Hawaii, to Australia, to Washington state, to Southern California. But again and again he returned to the City by the Bay. It was there that he began autofellating onstage, won the title "Biggest Dick in San Francisco," and launched his five-year career in gay porn video.

In 1989 he realized that a purple mark on his calf, which he had taken for a motorcycle exhaust pipe burn, was a Kaposi's Sarcoma lesion. He bought forty-seven acres of land in rural Wisconsin and named it Littledick. . . .

All of which territory Scott covered in *Autopornography: A Memoir of Life in the Lust Lane.* But that book left off just when Scott's life grew even more interesting—with the advent of the pioneering journal he published and edited for four years: *STEAM,* "The Literate Queer's Guide to Sex and Controversy."

STEAM was highly influential and is sorely missed. It went down with *wilde,* a glossy porn magazine Scott tried to launch—bankrupting him in the midst of protracted battles with lymphoma and an ex-lover named Larry.

It is a testament to Scott's character that losing *STEAM* did not destroy him. On the contrary, he became more productive than ever. He appeared on stage in a play based on his experiences in porn. He authored *Autopornography.* He penned the weekly columns that grew into this book. And, most importantly to him, he wrote his own play, *Ex-Lovers,* and saw it staged at Theatre Rhinoceros in San Francisco.

In June 1997 he wrote me: "Words cannot express how elated I am right now. We're talking, here, about one of my major Lifetime Goals: having a play of mine produced. The past two years have seen the realization of two others: acting professionally in a play (however minor & tawdry) and getting my first book published. Steve, I'm running out of Goals! Really, I'm not complaining; I'm just wondering, Where do I go from here? How could life get any better?"

*   *   *

Scott's title for this book refers to a famous line from *The Importance of Being Earnest*: "The truth is rarely pure and never simple." But I must protest that there was indeed a certain purity about Scott. And there was a beautiful simplicity in the gospel he preached: "Sex is wholesome and natural. It doesn't need to be hidden. It won't harm the children. It's not an assault. It's a declaration of membership in the human race."

This is not, however, to suggest that Scott was uncomplicated. Elsewhere in this book he tells us: "Sex is unimportant. Trivial, unnecessary, frivolous and boring."

"I'm tired of being Scott O'Hara," he complained to the *Bay Area Reporter* in the last month of his life. "I hate to rewrite history, but I wonder how much I actually enjoyed [sex]. I think I liked the idea of sex more than the actual act." He added: "I've become practically a Puritan."

That claim can be questioned.

A big-dicked porn star's ambivalence about living up to his public image is but one of the many fascinating subjects Scott expounds on in this quintessentially O'Haran work. In *Rarely Pure and Never Simple,* the most seasoned of his writings, Scott treats us to rhapsodies about the erotic potentials of impotence, leather jackets, hospital waiting rooms, and rimming sea anemones. He rails against cigarette smokers, gym queens, size queens, and "gay-for-pay" pornstars. He gives us the dirt on *Making Porn.* He shares his fantasy of being anally penetrated by the head of a bald man. And, with inimitable style, he defends promiscuity, unsafe sex, intergenerational love, and walls perforated by fist-sized holes.

Scott was never one to shy from controversy. But with his final book he managed to become even more audaciously honest. It was I who urged Scott to publish *Autopornography* with The Haworth Press, but one thing that bugged me a little about that book was the voice. Having met Scott in person, I found myself slightly puzzled by the "Hey, guys" bravado he sometimes affected in print. That wasn't the way Scott talked. His voice was conventionally masculine, but there was a gentlemanly refinement and politesse to his speech. This comes across better here.

The blunt and shocking truth is that Scott O'Hara was eminently *decent.*

But I had better stop there or else he really will come back and haunt me.

Anyone who reads this book and knew this remarkable man, even from afar, is sure to smile and nod (or grimace and shake their head), and say, "That's Scott."

*   *   *

There is another change of address postcard tacked to my bulletin board. Adorned with an image of Scott autofellating, it includes an invitation to write the executor of his will to request a fragment of his cremated remains ("one final chance to 'do with him what you will' "). It reads: "Scott 'Spunk' O'Hara wishes to announce his final relocation. If you ever find yourself in the vicinity, do drop in for a visit."

Steven Zeeland

Do Be Fruitful, Won't You Dear?

The appellations we've acquired never cease
to make me giggle at the miscommunication.
The ones who hurl these epithets, like spears,
clearly think of them as insults: "Fairies! Queers!"
For most of history, the fairy—in whatever guise—
was neither feared nor taunted, but respected;
and Queer's a term that certainly applies—
I wouldn't want to play a "normal" role.
But Fruit's the word that really gets me rolling.
I take it with a certain sense of irony
that many of my favorite things should be
drippy, firm and fleshy, sweet and juicy,
a solace to this sometimes-troubled soul of mine:
whether meaning pears or men, a Fruit's divine.

Sunday, December 15, 1996

The Truth Is ...

STEAM Magazine, which I edited and published for three years, was an ivory tower for me. I told my partner when we started, "I don't want to have anything to do with anything remotely business-like. You handle distribution and money and printing and all those other quotidians. I'll handle making the magazine something we can be proud of." This proved a source of tension between us over the years, as "something we can be proud of" meant very different things to us. I was talking about literary qualities; he was thinking of dollar signs. Funny, since I was the one who put up the money in the first place . . . but then, money has never been entirely "real" to me. That's what comes of having too much of it for your own good.

After *STEAM* folded (and *Wilde,* too, which had completely drained that bottomless pit of money) I was left somewhat aimlessly casting about for something constructive to do with my talents, between writing *Autopornography* and my first play, *Ex-Lovers.* A friend suggested writing newspaper columns. Hey, sounded good to me; I'm a pretty opinionated kind of guy, so I figured I could ruffle some feathers, at least. I dashed off half a dozen and sent them out to about fifty gay papers around the country. I think I heard back from ten of them; six papers eventually printed one or more of my columns. Oh, I did some follow-up calling and badgering of editors, but the truth is, I've never been good at selling my work. It's that money thing again: I don't like even talking about it. And it's kind of hard for me to believe that people really want to read what I have to say. Call it an inferiority complex, and don't laugh. Even the Scott O'Haras of the world have them.

Still, there were two papers—*On the Wilde Side,* on Long Island, and *Pittsburgh's OUT*—that ended up running columns for an entire year. At that point, *OtWS* folded, and I lost interest in being a columnist. Too many other things on my plate, and not enough marketing skills. Syndicating a column, I discovered, is a full-time job . . . and I really didn't feel like giving a 50 percent cut to an agent.

What was more interesting, though, was the papers that declined to run them. The editors I talked to had various reasons, of course, but several of them said, "Sorry, we can't use four-letter words." I must confess, that shocked me. Can't say "dick" in a gay paper? Oh, dear. We're in trouble.

Most of these columns talked about dick. Talked about it in theory, if not in fact. Mused about why it is that we can't talk about it, and why it should be so important in our lives. These are the things that fascinate me most, these days. A nice rousing public debate over the propriety of dick-pictures in the window of a bookstore is more interesting to me, I'm afraid, than the thought of going out and sucking some real live dick. How the mighty have fallen. I do feel that I got just as much pleasure from writing these essays as I ever did from my "field research" for *STEAM*. These pieces were the kernel of this book (and a few of them were expanded into longer pieces for other purposes). Some of them will undoubtedly offend you. Tough shit. None of my writing has ever been about winning friends in high places, and I make no apologies for these essays.

A Dick by Any Other Name

One of the most frequent, and annoying, questions that I'm asked by my adoring public is, "Is Scott O'Hara your real name?" Annoying, because yes, I know what they mean by that question, but it presupposes a whole set of societal values that I don't accept. For instance: That parents have the right (or ability) to create and/or define their children. My parents gave me a name at birth; it was not Scott O'Hara. It was someone else's name. You see, they thought they had produced a nice christian baby who would get married and settle down on the farm next to theirs and pass on their values to his children. So they gave me a name that suited such a destiny. Need I add, I was not thrilled. I knew from a very early age that I was a changeling. I spent the next eighteen years looking for my real name, and since I found it I have not pretended to be anyone else.

(Not quite true. When I was working for Falcon, well, they insisted on knowing my *real* real name. They would never have believed me if I'd told them Scott O'Hara was my real name, nor would they have allowed me to use it. They insist on anonymity for their stars. So I came up with a different birth certificate. I didn't let them call me Danny, however.)

This all sounds much more mystical and magical than I normally get, but the fact is, names are powerful. Mine is more so than most, perhaps, because more people know it. Saying "Scott O'Hara" to someone is likely to set off a train of associations—whether accurate or not. The reason I object to the practice of pornstars inventing "screen names" is that it creates a false image, a misleading persona; it disconnects the "public" image from the private one, so that what we see up on the screen is only a fraction of a person. A "porn name" only refers to a person's sexuality and doesn't even do a very good job of representing that. Well, okay, fine, I hear you say: That's all we're interested in. If true, I feel that's a pity. I know it's not true for me. The porn films that I think are most successful—the ones that turn me on the most—are the ones that try to integrate the performers' sexuality with the rest of their lives, the ones that show us how sex really works. Sex is never isolated, cut off from the rest of life. And seeing a real person—with a real name, real emotions, and real pimples—is more sexy, to me, than seeing a glamorous pornstar with a name like Dirk Dixon having what Erica Jong called "zipless sex."

When the subject of porn comes up in conversation, the most common critique I hear is that the men in these videos aren't "real." Of course they're not; they're fabrications of the movie studios, created by a gym, a tanning studio, and a plastic surgeon. The nom de porn is just the appropriate finishing touch for such a mannequin. (Have we had a pornstar yet named "Ken Doll"? No, I suppose that would be just too obvious.) Directors and producers will tell us, helplessly shrugging their shoulders, "We only produce what the public wants!" But the (quite informal) surveys I've conducted would indicate just the opposite: That there is a market for more "real" porn, with more average-looking men, men who you might realistically expect to encounter on the street. Naturally, my survey is skewed: These respondents are all friends of mine, and therefore have exquisite taste and prodigious intellectual powers.

There was a time when not all pornstars considered it essential to take pseudonyms. Richard Locke never did, to the best of my knowledge, nor did Chris Burns. There was something in this straightforward honesty that impressed me, and still does: These were men who weren't ashamed of their sex lives, who considered it the most natural thing in the world to have their dicks and butts up there on a movie screen. But sometime in the mid-1980s, the attitude changed. I don't quite understand why; maybe it had something to do with the proliferation of "straight" performers in gay roles (another phenomenon I don't understand). The reasons given always have to do with public exposure: What if my parents found out? What if my boss found out? What if I run for political office in ten years? I don't think any of these hold much water, but then, I've never been a big fan of closets. We recently had a graphic example of a pornstar being "outed" and losing his job and his wife; performing under a pseudonym didn't seem to help him much. Maybe he should have worn a mask, too, and gotten the studios to use one of those audio distortion machines on his voice.

I don't know what this particular performer has decided to do with himself, now that his cover is blown. If he does, in fact, consider himself straight, I should think it would be dreadfully tiresome for him to make a full-time career of gay porn. But if he does, my advice to him would be: Drop the silly screen name. Drop the façade. Whatever your real name is—and that's for you to decide—use it. Give us a person, not a persona. You might be surprised by how popular it proves to be.

Making Porn: The Hangover

Have you ever known someone so tacky, so completely declassé, that when her dildo disappeared, she immediately accused you of stealing it? I thought not. (For those of you who answered "yes," you have my condolences.) With luck, I'll never know another one.

I was an actor manqué in high school; I've always dreamed of being on the professional stage. (My jack-off career, though very enjoyable, doesn't quite count. Equity never noticed me.) So when Ronnie Larsen suggested that I really ought to go onstage in his new play, *Making Porn* (which was, after all, based on scenes from my porn career, which I'd narrated to him in half a dozen endless telephone calls), there was no way I could resist the lure.

Ronnie's method of interviewing is somewhat unusual: He asks a question, listens to a few seconds of the response, and then proceeds to answer the question in his own words for the next five minutes.

The first time I met Ronnie was in May, when he and his producer, a toad named Caryn, and one of their friends drove up to Wisconsin to do a reading of the new play. (They were in rehearsal in Chicago at the time.) I admit, I wasn't altogether thrilled with the script. My immediate reaction: If he ever gets to Hollywood and starts writing sitcoms, he'll be a smash. But hey, his last play (which was certainly no more distinguished) ran for five months. You can argue with success if you want to, but it won't get you very far. I said yes.

Our next encounter was in San Francisco, in July, at the first rehearsal. Still missing two of the actors, but we went ahead with it. I don't recall much of the early rehearsals. They went well; Ronnie was easygoing, congenial, and Caryn was seldom present. But we had less than three weeks of rehearsal time, and as the opening night came nearer, Ronnie became a certifiable maniac. He began exploding every time one of us said a word wrong. His script was the *gospel*, goddammit, and he didn't choose his words casually, he put blood, sweat and tears into it. . . . My favorite moment came when he spent half an hour lecturing us on the difference between "porn" and "porno," and why it was so important that on page 17, line 10, we say porn, while on the next page we should say porno. I felt like saying, "Ronnie, Auden is dead. He's not going to be in the audience."

Ronnie blew several gaskets over that last week, and even ended up canceling opening night. Said we needed another week of previews. He also refused to invite the reviewers, saying he'd be embarrassed to have a show this bad reviewed. Real encouraging ego boosts, huh? Mind you, the audiences loved us. We got triple curtain calls from the very first night; it was always sold out. Ronnie never got around to inviting the critics, so we were never reviewed—which, for some of us, was the unkindest cut of all. I'd never had a "legitimate" notice before; I was looking forward to that. And for the woman in the cast, who was a professional actress, it was the main reason she accepted the part.

So for the next two months we packed 'em in. It was only a sixty-seat theater; some nights I think there were seventy-five people there, which was a tight squeeze. Chairs in the aisles. It was a good feeling. And lest you think that the actors shared in Ronnie and Caryn's good fortune: They paid me $20 a week. That's for six shows a week, mind you. Ronnie also made me a deal, privately: Since the show was entirely based on my experiences, he said he'd pay me $100 a month for the next ten months. "Royalties." And still not a lot, considering the kind of dough that they were raking in. Well, I expect you can guess how much of that money I ever saw.

We were all relieved when, after the second week, Ronnie and Caryn had to go back to Chicago to close their show there. They didn't come back till closing week, and the show improved immensely in their absence. We all felt much freer.

What didn't amuse me was that when she left, Caryn took with her the lobby photo that I'd provided. She left me a note, saying she'd taken it for publicity purposes. I didn't have another print of that photo, and I didn't see any reason why I should make the photographer print another one. I told Caryn I wanted it back. She ignored me. Three weeks later—three weeks with a blank space on the wall where my photo was supposed to be—I demanded it back. She ignored me. That Friday, I let the stage manager know I wasn't going on Saturday if I didn't have my lobby photo back. Now, divadom really doesn't come naturally to me. Maybe my life would be easier if it did. But I felt that I'd been pushed beyond the limits of civility. Playing to packed houses for three weeks and not having my photo up in the lobby—that's outrageous.

Friday and Saturday were not good days for me. I wasn't looking forward to canceling the show. I do believe in that old stage dictum. But fortunately, after various acrobatics by the stage manager (who did a heroic job of managing Caryn), my photo reappeared, only slightly the worse for wear. From then on, all was sweetness and light and harmony among the dressing room divas.

Still . . . by closing night, I don't think anyone was sorry to see it fold. Two months is a long time to be corralled backstage with five other temperamental actors.

The final insult didn't come until a couple of weeks after closing. I got my final check (which proved to be, in fact, my *final* check) . . . for $81.30, or some such amount. Caryn had provided an itemized bill: $120, minus $24 for those "comp" tickets I had requested, minus $14.70 for the dildo that I'd taken from the dressing room . . . excuuuse me? Now, yes, there were a couple of dildoes used in the play (well, "displayed," not used—don't get the wrong idea). When Caryn had originally produced them, I'd laughed, because they were the most ridiculous-looking dildoes I'd ever seen, all floppy and droopy. Nothing I'd ever allow in *my* dildo collection. Which I had told Caryn, in no uncertain terms. Which was why I was so offended by Caryn's assumption that I'd stolen them. I called her up, in L.A., and blazed at her for a few minutes: "I know *you're* in the habit of stealing things left and right," I said, "but that doesn't mean I am." And that, predictably, was the last I ever heard from her or Ronnie. They've gone on to produce the play all over the country, for the past two years. I am informed, by someone who managed the Chicago production, that they've cleared well over a million bucks off of it. I do have occasional fantasies about suing them. Since they clearly breached their contract with me (and I do have written proof of it) I could probably claim a percentage of the profits. But then I come to my senses. Yeah, I probably could; and so what? It would purely be for revenge, and I abhor the very idea. I don't *like* revenge. I don't ever want to be the kind of person who obsesses over every wrong that's ever been done to him; the Count of Monte Cristo and Sweeney Todd are not good role models. And I don't want or need the money. Much better to forget about it, to the best of my ability, and go on with my life. The assurance that I will never have to deal with either Ronnie or Caryn again should be payment enough for anyone.

Am I bitter about this experience? Yes. I don't think there's any point in trying to hide *that* from the perceptive reader. This was my stage debut; it should have been a fairy tale, right? And indeed, the glowing comments that I got from men on the street (which I continue to get) were the sort of sunshine in which every actor loves to bask. And I suppose it's good that I learned so quickly, and vividly, the downside of being in a play. Would I act again? Well, not if Ronnie or Caryn were connected with it, that much I can say for damn sure—and not without a written contract. Dealing with those two made me look back on my days in front of the camera with nostalgia. The process of making porn, I'm afraid—even the schlocky scenes depicted in the play, even "the milk bit" in which the actor is doused with a cold milk "cumshot"—was a far, far more pleasant procedure than the process of *Making Porn*. And in all my years of fucking for money, I never met a producer or director as slimy and unscrupulous as that pair.

Seeing Beauty

I have a photo on my desk of the most beautiful man I have ever met. No, he's not a Nordic god, with a cleft chin and muscles for days; he's a scrawny little runt of a guy, with a face that looks slightly simian. But he has the deepest, most liquid, understanding eyes it has ever been my misfortune to get lost in, and when he speaks, watching his lips move is easily the most sensuous experience of my life. These two features—eyes and lips, which can be lumped together under the general heading of "soul"—comprise my main standards of Beauty.

How these standards get formed is a question that has always puzzled me. Most of the men who ring my bell are one type or another of Latin: Mexican, Puerto Rican, Brazilian, Italian, Greek. (I don't think the Greeks consider themselves Latin, but there's a close affinity.) Did I grow up around any of these nationalities? No. To the best of my knowledge, the first time I ever saw a Mexican man was when I went on a whale-watching trip to Baja, California, when I was sixteen. The rest of the passengers may have been watching whales; I was watching the Mexican fishermen who sailed the boat. Grungy and poverty-stricken, they were nevertheless constantly laughing and smiling, and they were the most heart-stoppingly beautiful men I'd ever seen. I'll always regret being unable to work up the courage to proposition them.

But if this was my first encounter with the Latin male, where did my attraction originate? I don't have an answer, unfortunately. I certainly don't believe in such a thing as Objective, Absolute Beauty: These men are not equally attractive to everyone, obviously. In fact, the stereotype of The Beautiful Man, as sketched above, is almost diametrically opposite. And my eyes are not closed to such beauty. I can appreciate the blond, blue-eyed beauties in the Macy's ads. But it's the sight of a field full of migrant Mexican farmworkers that almost makes me run my motorcycle off the road.

Unsurprisingly, I was once accused of stereotyping these men. A man of Italian descent claimed, in indignant tones, that I was perpetuating the popular notion of Italian men as nothing but sex gods. He missed the point, I think. *All* men are sex gods: That is to say, all men are sexual. Different men are attractive to each of us. It would be disingenuous (and extremely unhealthy and dishonest) to claim that all men are equally attractive. But I doubt that there is any man in the world who is not attractive to *somebody*. Beauty is always an individual standard. I sometimes think that the problems of the world would be solved if we could somehow mix up the world's skin color like we mix a can of paint, mandating that every child born shall have parents of different races; in one generation, we would have no more black, no more white. Just a nice, even mocha. Perhaps it would alleviate racial tension, but it would be a sad day for those of us who find black men, or Nordic blonds, particularly irresistible. And I'm sure that another caste system would immediately be invented to replace race. People seem to have an inherent need for such distinctions.

I went, last weekend, to Los Angeles, and met a man who rivals the photo of the Greek boy on my desk. The eyes, the lips, the smile . . . I could have spent hours just staring. He probably doesn't think of himself as beautiful. Mexicans do not get a lot of positive reinforcement for their looks, especially in Southern California, where many people regard them as an overgrown species of cockroach. Now, I'm not a big fan of Los Angeles, and I don't go there very often, but every time I do, I am overwhelmed with lust. I stand on a streetcorner, waiting to cross, and my heart starts hammering in my chest at the sight of a group of middle-aged men hanging out in front of an auto-body shop. I wish I could tell them how beautiful they are. Fortunately, it doesn't seem to matter to them. It's plain from the smiles on their faces that they're in love with life, regardless of how they're viewed by the WASPs who employ them. And maybe that's the real definition of Beauty, the thing that makes me melt inside: The sight of a man who sees the joy in life, and who isn't afraid to show it. And this, I think, is a very Latin characteristic.

Whaddya Like?

That's a question I get asked a lot. Everyone wants to know what a famous sex star likes to do in his private life. Trouble is, I find it almost impossible to answer, in concrete terms. What people want to hear, simple answers such as "I like to fuck," or "I like to be tied up and pissed on," simply don't apply. Yeah, I like those things, and a hundred other sex acts too, but the things that really matter to me are less quantifiable. I can sum them up in a few words, but the answer doesn't satisfy most people.

Enthusiasm. That's numero uno. I like being with a guy who likes what he's doing—whatever that might be. When a guy sticks his butt up in the air and starts moaning when my tongue gets in there, I like to know that he's not doing it just because he thinks it's what I want. I've never gotten any pleasure out of forcing guys to do things they don't really want to do.

Second on my list is Intimacy. This makes a lot of people look at me a little funny, since I'm also known as a vigorous defender of anonymous sex, sex in parks, bathhouse sex. What people don't understand is that some of my best sex may be anonymous—but it's almost never the cold, emotionless type of sex that so many people associate with the bushes. Kissing is important to me: A man who doesn't want to kiss is unlikely to get my motor going. (That doesn't mean that he has to actually DO it. I met a man recently who obviously was aching to kiss me, but who was so devoted to his Safer Sex principles that he wouldn't open his mouth. That was one of the hottest encounters I've ever had. Seeing the desire in his eyes as he stroked my face really stoked my fire.) And smiling, laughing, sharing: I like a man who doesn't deny the pleasure he's getting from the act. The butch, unemotional number may look hot on the street, but he seldom finds his way into my bed.

And that's the third quality that I look for in a man, even more difficult than the first two to define: Joy. Men with a sparkle in their eyes, men who can see the pleasure and beauty in everyday life, men who can face even tragedy and laugh. I've been criticized, often, for my flip attitude about AIDS. People say I don't take it seriously enough, that I encourage unsafe sex because I don't tear my hair and wail about how horrible my life is since I got infected. Well, no. I don't. My life's been pretty damn wonderful this past decade, and I'm happy to tell people that. And I like playing with guys who are equally able to seek out silver linings.

Okay, I'll admit that I also notice other things, when I see a man on the street. A nice pair of pecs does catch my attention, and a shaved head always turns mine. Any face that looks like it came from south of the border can start my maracas rattling. But I'm not kidding when I say that the first thing I notice about a man, and the thing that makes me want to get to know him, is what shows in his eyes. Joy; Intimacy; Enthusiasm. These are the things that turn me on. And when I'm turned on by a person, there are very few limits on what I like to do.

Where There's a Wall,
There's a Way

No—leave the wall. Remember, you must always leave the wall.

Tom Jones

Much of the five years I spent in rural Wisconsin was spent building walls. Quite literal walls, stone walls for my rock gardens, incorporating probably fifty tons of stone and thousands of plants— an impressive project, quite labor-intensive, and immensely satisfying. Winter was a time of hibernation, of sitting back and reviewing the accomplishments of the year, and of writing. I loved the separation of seasons into discrete activities: Being indoors in summer was intolerable, being outdoors in winter was impracticable. This division gave me the chance to anticipate the changing of the seasons in a way that no Californian will ever know. I likened it to having four different rooms in my house, with totally different furnishings and views: A chance to change my environment without actually moving. And I loved that separation.

Some psychotherapists would undoubtedly nod wisely at my obsession with building stone walls and make notes in their little notebooks. Why did I do it? Well, I tried to explain that, years ago, in an article called "Rockwalls and Sex." I don't think I did a very good job. Building those walls, in a sense, filled the same place in my life that sex had when I lived in San Francisco: It gave me a glow of fulfillment, a sense of pride. Spending an evening jerking off onstage roused many of the same emotions, for me, as spending a day fitting rocks together. The difference is that the rock walls were still standing the next year. (Most of them still are.) Getting my rocks off, while satisfying to both me and my audiences, did not have the same sense of accomplishment. So . . . I took to the country, and began "walling off the world."

Walls have a bad rep. Most people prefer to tear them down. I think they can be the most beautiful structures we ever create. They allow surprises; they give us the chance for discovery. When I discovered my first glory hole in a bathroom wall, I can't tell you how awed and impressed I was with the ingenuity of some nameless proto-architect, the man who had realized the potential inherent in a bathroom stall. What glory, indeed! And none of it would be possible without the wall. Without walls, the mystery that makes glory-hole sex possible would melt like a late spring snow, and we would be left with unenhanced Reality. Would we be healthier, mentally, for this tearing-down of the walls? Arguably; but life would be less interesting. We need to have these divisions in our lives, these distinctions: A is not B. I am not you. Straight is not gay. That dick sticking through the partition is, undoubtedly, attached to a man, but the man is choosing to remain unknown, anonymous, "Other." His dick is all I really know of him, and that's quite enough. I can picture the man in any way I want, if I want, or I can just enjoy the dick on its own merits, like a beautiful bronze sculpture mounted on a museum wall, without worrying about the man behind it.

Where am I going with this? Well might you ask. I am, after all, the fanatical advocate of tearing down all the closet doors, of exposing all your innermost secrets to the world; I've said, time and again, that keeping secrets is unhealthy. What is a wall besides a way of keeping a secret? There is a difference, however. Closets are maintained out of fear; walls are built for fun and functionality. When you decide that you're not going to tear down a particular wall—between rooms in your house, between seasons, between you and another person—you're giving your life more options for mystery, surprise, adventure, anticipation. You're preserving the spice of life. These marriage counselors who insist that relationships must be a complete melding of two people, with no walls between them—well, I think they miss the point. I suppose you can live like that, but I doubt that it's essential. In fact, sharing all of the rooms of your life with one other person is the quickest route I can think of to boredom.

Whereas the allure of peering over a wall—or around it, or through a glory hole—is a surefire interest-piquer. Walls are not impermeable. You can get around them. But tearing them all down is not the answer.

GWM, 35, Horizontal, Versatile, Asleep

I think age can be most effectively measured—quite poetically, too—as the hour at which sleep becomes more important than sex. I can remember a time in my life when that time was 8 a.m. It gradually retreated; today, it's more like 9 p.m. That's a frightening thought: You'd think that would imply late-middle age, at the very least, and yet I'm barely thirty-five. And when a date gets amorous at 10 p.m., after dinner and a play, all I can say is "I've got a headache."

Thus, yet another reason to patronize the baths. There are many reasons, but my favorite is that in a well-designed bathhouse there are always places to doze off . . . and be awakened after a refreshing nap, if fortune smiles, to find a sexy man doing interesting things to your body. He won't be offended if you continue to snore; whether feigned or real, your slumber can be incorporated into his fantasy. (Haven't you always wanted to ravish Sleeping Beauty, roll him over and leave him pregnant and still asleep?)

I was treated to just such a scenario recently: I'd decided to spend an afternoon at the baths, and I started with a peaceful snooze in the video room. Before going to sleep, I had taken time to pacify my throat with just one dick, belonging to a straight-looking young man wearing brown underwear, who shot a healthy load down my throat. I laid down, after he'd gone his way, with perfect assurance that I wouldn't sleep the whole day through.

And sure enough, after barely an hour of rest, a man's mouth aroused me. In both senses of the word. I lay there with eyes closed. I've not known many men who could get me hard by sucking me. It's not my biggest turn-on, but somehow the fact that I wasn't overtly responding to his ministrations made my dick respond more freely. And when he'd gotten me about as hard as he could reasonably expect to get me, he unwrapped a rubber, rolled it down my dick, and mounted me as easy as you please (having first ripped the seat of his underwear, which I thought a charming touch).

Now, I know you're skeptical: Did I maintain my faux-repose through all these contortions? Well, until my dick was well inside him, yes, I did. I don't think I fooled him, but at least I let him do the work. Once he was well-mounted, however, I started thrusting, and he couldn't have liked it more. Didn't take him long to shoot his load, and a good thing, too, because my dick was starting to deflate. Being sheathed in rubber does that. Can't seem to feel a thing through the damn things. I felt like I was doing a Public Service Announcement, or giving succor to the needy. But making someone cum always cheers me up; after he withdrew and took the rubber and himself away, I drifted back to sleep, smiling.

It was probably an hour or so later that the same boy returned— still wearing the same torn brown underwear. This time I felt his fingers probing around my ass. Okay, there might have been a time in my life when I was casual enough about being fucked to just let him in; let me rephrase that, I can vividly remember such times. But not today. Today I need lots of loosening up. Blame it on AIDS, blame it on hemorrhoids, blame it on what you will. And I tend to bleed if the guy is too rough, which causes queasiness in many of my partners. So continuing to feign sleep was not an option. I spread my legs welcomingly, pulled him down on top of me, arranged my towel under my butt, and whispered in his ear, "You'll have to be real gentle." He was. He wore a rubber at first, but sometime during the course of the fuck, presumably when he pulled out to jerk off for a while, he lost it. I didn't notice for some time, and when I did, I was delighted. He had extraordinary stamina (this might have had something to do with having cum twice already that afternoon) and I eventually had to ask him to hurry it up, my ass was wearing out. And he asked me, twice, if I wanted his load up my butt; and I assured him, twice, that I did, and he shot. Hallelujah.

And then—need I add?—I went back to sleep. At six o'clock, when I checked out, it all seemed like no more than a glorious, sensual, passion-soaked dream. But I felt wonderfully rested; and there was a pair of torn brown underwear under my towel.

Playing with My Mind

For years, I've referred to it in my journal as "fake-fucking." I hate that term. There's nothing fake about it. It can be as real, as intense, as exciting, as any other type of fucking. But I don't know what else to call it. It's not frottage; it seldom even leads to climax. It's not about orgasm, but about control, and suspense, and lots of other intangibles.

What I'm talking about is having a man on top of me—a man who likes being on top of me, and who understands how much I need to be dominated, controlled, subdued. This doesn't mean that he spits in my face and calls me his worthless slave. If he did, I'm afraid I'd start giggling. It's all a lot more subtle than that. He holds me down; he rubs himself against me; he stares into my eyes, and I'd swear he reads my thoughts. He tells me, sometimes in graphic detail, how he's *going* to fuck me. I've got a vivid imagination; when he says he's going to fuck me, I can feel his dick sliding into me, and my body goes into spasms. Sometimes, he'll flip me over onto my stomach and rub his dick up and down my buttcrack. This really makes me crazy. I'm moaning, shoving my butt up every time he slides; jabbering "Put it in put it in put it in!" And if he's really, *really* good . . . he won't. I don't meet a lot of men who are this good at torture. Okay, there's no doubt about it: I like to get fucked. Really fucked. But the intensity that builds up from a prolonged roller-coaster of anticipation—the frenzy, and cooling-down periods, and starting all over again—is more exciting, to me, than the physical plunge of dick into ass.

I met such a man the other day. Of course, I didn't know it when I met him; all I knew was that he had good eyes. That's usually a good sign. Eyes that looked directly at me, eyes that were open wide and seemed to take it all in. Once in bed, he never stopped watching my face. He never stopped smiling, either, even when his face was twisted up in ecstasy. And when he started "fucking" me, his words were enough to reduce me to a quivering, moaning, mass of jelly. I go off into another space entirely when I'm like that: My face turns wild and frantic, my eyes go blank, I wouldn't be surprised if I sometimes foam at the mouth. He clearly liked watching all of this. I could see him smiling, as he told me what he was going to do to me (and felt my body jerking underneath his at every word). I was a puppet, and he was pulling my strings expertly, as if he'd made me. Remarkable, when you consider that I'd only met him two days earlier. Some men do have that ability. It's admirable.

No, he didn't actually stick his dick inside me. He didn't need to. We both knew what we wanted, and he was good enough at puppeteering that the actual act wasn't necessary. Oh, he promised me that next time we get together, he'll do it. Maybe he will; maybe that was just another part of the act, another way to make me moan (it did). I don't think I'm the only one in the world who appreciates the erotic value of frustration; being told, "I'm going to fuck you—next Monday" is enough to drive me stark raving mad.

And after all this was over, after he'd sprayed his cum everywhere, shaking and jerking, as I twisted his tits, and then he rolled over next to me ("safest" sex I've had in years, probably)—I lay there, basking in the warmth and comfort of his body next to me, and I knew without any doubt: I've been *fucked.* By a master. There's that certain glow that comes from having had a man's dick plunging deep inside you, possessing you, owning you; knowing that I've satisfied such a man is one of my greatest thrills. I don't think this is news to any of you. What you might not have realized however, is that with some men the physical act isn't necessary. I don't suppose it would really matter if these men had dicks at all. It has more to do with the eyes, and the words, and the ability to take control. I guess it has more in common with hypnotism than with sex.

Come to think of it, this whole process could be described as S/M—though I seldom go very far into that world. But the sense of control, of leaving someone unsure of what's coming next, of instilling just a *touch* of fear, is one of the hallmarks of all the best Masters. What it is—and unfortunately this term has been used so widely that it's no longer specific enough—is a mind-fuck. Mind-fucking is not acknowledged, by the authors of *The Joy of Gay Sex,* as a specific sex act; please don't let them know about it. Let it remain on the edge: Nameless, undefined, and slightly dangerous. It works better that way.

Schloop, Spooge, Spunk:
A Syntax of Sex

"What's the hardest part of writing porn?" people ask me. For-going the obvious double entendre, I prefer the more literal, "Learning to type with one hand."

In reality, porn writing doesn't differ noticeably from other forms of writing. You still need to observe all the basic rules (at least, to the extent that you want people to understand you; William S. Burroughs didn't worry about such technicalities, and he seems to have done all right). The problem is that some writers seem to forget the basics, figuring it's "just porn—no one will notice." And, well, they may be right, but it's my contention that porn doesn't have to be "just porn." It can be great writing, too, and why not? Hence, a few reminders:

- Give your readers some credit. They've got imaginations. Give them some exercise. It's my contention that anyone who reads a book, even the most basic of books, has to have an imagination. The others are watching videos. So let them romp a little bit. Just because it's porn doesn't mean that you have to tell them everything. Sometimes implication is more titillating than description.
- Words are everything. Hey, that's all you've got, when you're writing porn: Only words. Use them. Use them all. Your fellow pornographers (and many readers) will undoubtedly snicker at the more exotic usages—you know, "throbbing man-spear," and so forth—but the fact is, seeing the word "dick" repeated sixteen times on one page is even more grating. No matter how much you fetishize jockstraps, there's only a certain number of times you can read the word before it loses all meaning. And while we're on the subject—I know there are many people out there who object to the nouveau-coinage of

"cum," as either a verb or noun, to describe that ultimate product of pornography. I'm not one of them. For chrissakes, folks, we've got few enough words in the English language that are specifically sexual, specifically intended to arouse: Prurient words. Cum is one of them. "Come" is a lame attempt to disguise porn as respectable writing; I can't read it without adding, mentally, "home, Lassie." "Cum" is charged with a different meaning, a practically primeval meaning. My appreciation of it is increased by the fact that the distinction is only obvious on the printed page: It is a purely literary invention. Use it. Use jism, too; or jiz, or jizzom, or jazz, or however you want to spell it; use spunk, and spooge, and all the other invented words you can come up with. If it sounds sexy to you, quite likely it will sound sexy to your readers. No one's written the stylebook for pornographers yet, so you're free to invent your own. "Glory hole" or "gloryhole"? You decide.

- Which brings us to the bottom line of porn: Write what turns you on. I never write a porn story unless I have a hard-on; I can't imagine doing so. If it doesn't even turn you on, how the hell do you expect to turn other people on? This doesn't mean that you have to write the same story, over and over. I keep coming up (not cumming up, thank you) with new fantasies every day. My basic rule is to follow my dick into a story. I don't plot it out in advance; I just keep trying to imagine what twist will turn me on the most. Usually it has something to do with the unexpected, the unusual, and often the irrelevant. Whenever I start getting too close to cumming (yes!), I always try to throw in a digression, something to slow the reader down, to puzzle him a little, maybe even infuriate him. Frustration is the biggest turn-on I can think of.

- Finally—and this is the point on which many, if not most, pornwriters really fall down: Don't lose your sense of humor. Sex is fun, for crying out loud—or at least, it should be. It's also frequently absurd, comical, and incredibly anticlimactic. I'm not saying that you have to make the sex in your stories as farcical as the sex you had last night; just remember that your basic function is as an entertainer. Sex is entertainment; so is humor. They mix remarkably well. There's a writer—no, I don't know his name—who has a particular trademark style, which includes the mention of "Lake Lothario" and "Olean-der Avenue." I've read entire books of his, waiting for the key words to show up; this man has a sense of humor about his writing, and he doesn't let it stand in the way of describing some real down and dirty, quirky, kinky sex. Is it literature? I'll leave that for the literary historians to decide. It sure makes me splooge.

Testament

People who know me from my legendary porn career, who are meeting me for the first time, will often say something along the lines of, "Gee, but you must be proud of having done those videos!" And I hardly know how to respond. Yes, and no. I don't spend a lot of time thinking about it. It's in my past, you understand, and while I'm certainly not ashamed of them, I have other things to occupy me now. When I think about them, yes, I do feel a burst of pleasure. That isn't very often, though. Every once in a while, though, something will happen to slap me in the face with it.

Last night, I was sucking a dick at a local sex club. It was an unusually large dick, extremely hard, with a slight upward curve. I'd sucked it at least once before, I knew: My throat was sending out recognition signals. (Pain! pain! pain!) I'm rather proud of my deep-throating abilities, but on the whole, I'd rather not test those limits, and this dick was a challenge. Still . . . I wasn't about to give up.

I speak so specifically about the dick, rather than the person, because I hadn't had a good look at the person. I was already flat on my stomach, you see, getting fucked within an inch of my life, when he knelt down in front of me and waved that instantly-familiar dick in my face. (His crotch hair—indeed, all his body hair—was trimmed short, which always emphasizes the essential strength and beauty of a vigorous boner.) And I sucked him—or, rather, he fucked my face—for possibly ten minutes; and he came. Delicious. I swallowed every drop, and kept nursing it, while the man on my back finished up and left. (I don't mean to minimize the fucker's expertise; he did a fabulous job, too.) Then I backed off and got to examine the guy a little more closely.

He had a shaved head—one of my biggest turn-ons these days, one which drives me absolutely wild with lust, one which makes me thankful to be a Modern Queerboy of the Nineties. His body hair, as mentioned, was clipped, but he obviously had a chest rug that would've done credit to a grizzly. Underneath that, he had muscles. Shoulders as wide as all of Montana, pecs that were like rocks, and a set of ridges on his stomach that were really impressive. The sort of guy who looks like he could pick you up and toss you over his shoulder without turning a hair. He also had a titring. No tattoos, though, somewhat to my surprise.

That's when he dropped the bombshell. Looking down at me, smiling, he said, "That's payback for all those loads I shot over Spunk, back in Midland, Texas, in 1985. For a queer punk trapped in a small town, you were an inspiration." And I went into shock. You see, here I'd been, worshipping this young god—I figure he was about twenty-eight—as the personification of the New Generation of Queerboys, which is exactly what he was . . . only to discover that I'd had a hand in making him what he became. I felt a shiver run through me, head to toe. Pride, yes; but also just simple amazement, that I could have done this. Without even having any knowledge of it, yet! Somehow, in my relative innocence, without any concept of what it would mean to the boys in Midland, I'd created a persona that gave them permission to rebel. Not just against their parents, mind you, but against the equally repressive cliches of gay society. As a man sows, so shall he reap: I created Spunk, the Queer Punk, and now here was this Vision of Queerdom shooting his spunk down my throat.

I don't get moments like this one very often. If I did, my head would swell to very unattractive proportions. I don't think I overestimate the importance of my career on the formation of these guys' libidos. Hey, lots of guys, even twenty-something Queerboys, have never seen a pornflick and couldn't care less. I agree with them that there are lots of things in life that are intrinsically more important than porno. But I'm extremely proud to have been able to broaden the range of choices available to them.

And my throat is sore this morning; but I feel vindicated, justified, in a way that is almost paternal. This is my Beloved Son, in whom I am well-pleased. God, I love the nineties.

Call Me Irresponsible

When he slipped his dick into me, he didn't ask me for permission. He knew I wanted it, he knew I was positive, and he wasn't looking for validation. Of course I could have stopped him, expressed concern for his health, asked him if he really wanted to take this risk . . . but frankly, I would consider questions like that to be insulting. This is a well-educated, thinking adult we're talking about, with a firsthand knowledge of AIDS; he knew the risks. He knew it was an act of rebellion, fucking without a condom, and it wasn't necessary to discuss it further. In other words: He was taking responsibility for his actions.

"Responsible" is a funny word. It's most commonly used, these days, to mean "someone who listens to what I have to say." Anyone who doesn't follow his doctor's advice, or who refuses to make his sex life "safe," or who uses recreational drugs, is called "irresponsible" by various segments of the population. They're not behaving the way they're "supposed" to behave. In another sense, they're behaving in an absolutely responsible fashion: They're making their own decisions, not trying to pass the buck. When I rim someone, I know there's a chance of my getting a parasite. Most parasites are easily treatable, but some are not. At least one of them can kill you. There was a time when this knowledge was enough to keep my tongue away from that inviting hole, but my priorities have changed, in recent years. I'm rimming again, enthusiastically, against all doctors' advice. I've already had one bout of amoebas. It wasn't fun, but, balanced against the pleasure I've gotten from eating ass, I think I'll continue. There are trade-offs in life. The definition of responsibility, for me, is accepting those risks and rewards as your own, rather than blaming someone else for them.

He was, shall we say, a vigorous fucker. He didn't hold back. After ten minutes of slamming, my asshole was feeling a little numb. That was the point when he pulled out and saw some traces of blood on his dick. Well, yeah: It's not uncommon for my ass to bleed a little, especially when it gets pounded like that. I assured him that I was fine. He said, "I'd better stop, though. I think I'm still negative, and I'd kinda like to stay that way."

Yes, I'll admit that I was a bit taken aback; surprised. I keep asking myself this question: If I were negative, would I fuck someone bareback who I knew was positive? The risk is probably minimal; no matter how cautious all the health experts insist on being, I find it hard to believe that very many guys have gotten infected from topping an infected bottom. Some, sure, but not a lot.

And then my mind drifts back, inevitably, to an incident fairly early in the epidemic: Say, twelve years ago. The PWA Coalition had just been founded, and I'd met one of its members—the first out, public AIDS activist I'd known. I liked him; we talked. And then he asked if he could suck my dick. I was petrified. Theoretically, I knew, it was low risk . . . but that doesn't help. I let him, for a minute or two. Nothing happened, of course, except that I got more and more freaked out, until I told him, "Sorry, I just can't do this." I never saw him again; he died about a year later. I feel sad, now, that I wasn't able to give him that simple pleasure.

How was I to know, then, that I'd eventually become one of the most outspoken proponents of Positive Sex?

Positives, by and large, have become aware of the consequences of their sex lives. (Am I over-generalizing, here? Let me revise that: The Positives I know tend to be more aware.) We've learned a lot of unpleasant facts about the effects of various behaviors: diet, lifestyle, and yes, sex habits. Sometimes, it seems appropriate to make changes. Negatives—well, for the most part, they haven't been faced with quite as many realities. They just have one choice in front of them: Do they want to stay Negative, and if so, What's It Worth? Some of them are so terrified of AIDS that they cut themselves off entirely from gay sex. Some "go straight," and get married. Some find a lover and count on monogamy to keep them "clean." I don't agree, obviously, but I respect their willingness to take responsibility for their own actions and desires. At least one person draws the line elsewhere—like, when he sees blood on his dick.

He finished up by jacking off, while I licked his balls. Shot a real impressive load. I licked some of it up; it was good. The cum of a man who knows what he wants, and what it's worth to him. The cum of an "irresponsible" man.

Better Than Sex

Okay, now I'm going to make a value judgment, and it's going to be one that will make a lot of you shake your heads sorrowfully, sure that I've finally gone off the deep end. Talking is better than sex.

Now that you've mentally confiscated my Queer Membership Card, let's go into the details. No, obviously, not all talking is better than all sex. Most talk bores me. I am an exceptionally quiet person, not easily drawn into conversation, and if I go an entire twenty-four hours without hearing the phone ring, I consider that a successful day. But sometimes—and here we get into the strongly subjective world of interpersonal relationships—sometimes I meet someone who truly fascinates me on a mental level, someone with whom I feel that legendary "bond," and all I really want to do with him is talk. And sometimes we can spend all night doing nothing else, just pouring out life stories, dreams, projects, fantasies—and I'll get up in the morning feeling like I've had a night of the best sex ever. It doesn't happen often, obviously. You can't take this much emotional intensity on a sustained basis. At least, I can't.

Well, okay, fine; but how does this relate/compare to sex? Well . . . sex, for me, has always been about communication. Sometimes it works; more often, especially with strangers, there are missed cues, misinterpreted signals, which lead to confusion and disappointment. Gay life is full of such symbols, going far beyond the basics of "the Hanky Code." We've got a legendary knack for spotting each other; this isn't psychic vibrations, just a complicated set of non-verbal cues that most of the world ignores. And when you meet someone who trips all your switches, there are probably preconceived notions in your head about what the two of you might do together. This can often lead to comical situations. Let's face it, that butch stud who takes you home and then throws his legs in the air is guilty of nothing more than mistaking his cues. And I have nothing against butch studs who like to get fucked; I find it very sweet, in

fact. But if I go home with someone expecting him to do the plow-
ing (and I usually do have such expectations), it can be frustrating
to learn that we've been talking different languages.

The process continues, of course. All through every sex act,
we're communicating with our partner: do this—no, more to the
left—please don't remove my tonsils. Most people, however, find it
somewhat embarrassing to express all these desires and preferences
verbally; they try to convey them with physical action. Shoving a
guy's head down to your crotch is a very effective means of communication; if he proceeds to bite you, that says something, too.
The problem, I find (and here I'm getting extremely subjective
again) is that a lot of guys aren't listening. I can't tell you how many
times I've been with a partner who didn't seem to be paying attention to all these subtle indications that I was in pain (screaming),
uncomfortable (wriggling), or just plain bored (snoring). And guess
what? That's why we have vocal cords. Talking—being open and
aboveboard and absolutely honest about what does and doesn't turn
you on, what you will or won't do—is really the best way of ensuring that you're on the same wavelength.

Admittedly, it's a very hot fantasy to imagine some stud who just
throws you down on the bed and does all the things to you that
you'd always wanted, without being asked. In reality, such a scenario would require, I think, a mind reader. Or at the very least, an
expert hustler, since hustling is primarily the art of knowing what
the customer wants before he knows he wants it. Maybe a long-term
lover—but some of the element of surprise is missing, in that case.

Now, as a writer, I ought to be an expert in the field of communication, right? In fact, often as not, I clam up and can't say what
needs to be said, whether that's "Fuck me harder!" or "Fuck off!"
A problem, I admit. So when I meet one of these studs who can
express himself as well verbally as physically, well, I feel like I've
found someone sorta special. I've got one at the moment. Oh, not
"got" as in, married, strangled, joined-at-the-hip, wedding-ringed;
but I've got him in every sense that's important to me. He talks to
me—and yes, he listens, too—and while I don't know all the details
of his life, he's probably the most communicative person I've met
in years. The other night, for whatever reason, I was feeling particularly horny and lonely, so I called him. He came over; we sat and

talked for about four hours, about sex, relationships, politics, friends, and food; and then he went home. I went to bed with the peaceful smile on my face that I used to think only came from being extremely well-fucked. Yes, it was "better than sex."

You could love a guy like that.

Why Is a Beach?

Tidepools. That was my first attraction to beaches. When I was a kid, we lived close enough to the Southern Oregon coast that we could take day trips. I encouraged them. Every time we went over to Brookings, I'd spend the day bending over tidepools, fascinated by the marine fauna: hermit crabs, sea anemones, starfish and barnacles—endless variety. My siblings had other entertainments: beachcombing, sunbathing, bodysurfing. I stayed happily absorbed in my underwater world. One of my favorite tricks was sticking my tongue into sea anemones, the ones that were close enough to the surface: They'd close up around my tongue, and their stinging felt like holding a nine-volt battery to the tongue. Besides, it made my sister go "Ewwww!" I view it, now, as my initiation into the art of rimming.

One thing I never recall doing, at that tender age, is lying on a towel.

Eventually, I grew up. More or less. By the time I was twenty, I had begun frequenting "beaches." The Belmont Rocks in Chicago, for example, which has no sand, and where swimming is not recommended (Lake Michigan's pretty polluted), but which does fulfill the primary requirement of a beach. Men. Nearly-naked men. Who were all there, near as I could tell, because all the rest of them were there. Don't think about it; it'll make your head ache. (What is the sound of one gay man on a beach? No one will ever know.) I still maintained a certain sense of the insanity of it all, knowing that a backyard, a park, or the roof of an apartment building would be vastly more convenient for most of these guys. But part of the joy of gay life, I eventually realized, comes from the sense of participation in one huge societal joke: Yes, we all know that we're behaving nonsensically, but it's all right, because we've all signed onto the Declaration of Style Over Substance. Everyone on the beach is delighted with the Emperor's new clothes—especially when the straights start buying them from us at greatly inflated prices.

Now, where was I, before I went off on a social-criticism riff? Beaches, oh yes. I got to Hawaii when I was twenty, found an apartment near the beach, and—well, what else?—became a terminal beach bum. Hung around Queen's Surf or Diamond Head all day; went to the baths at night if the action had been slow at Diamond Head. Rode my bicycle everywhere. Got a killer tan. (Just a figure of speech; no melanoma yet.) Smoked a lot of dope. Had to: That was the only way, at that age, to lie still long enough to do my tan any good. Hyperactive. Always had to be doing something: Swimming, cruising, riding my bicycle. I've got plenty of fragmentary memories from that period, and they're mostly good ones. Life was simple. But I still didn't understand the Why of a beach.

Couple years later, back in San Francisco, I finally found Land's End. Suddenly, I understood. It's a wilderness area within the city limits—at least, it was then. The park rangers have done their best to ruin it in the past decade: Building stairways, patrolling, etc. It's still pretty wild, though. And the reasons for going are still the same. Don't go for sun. You might get it, you might not. (Even on those rare days when downtown SF is blazing hot, you'll probably enter a fog bank at 30th Avenue.) Don't go for sex—ditto. I've had sex with hundreds of men there over the years, but there are also days when no one seems interested, and that's just fine. Sex is a bonus. If you go there expecting it, you're in trouble from the start.

No, what made me fall in love with Land's End was The Rock. There's a small beach, protected by headlands on either side, so that even on chilly days you can lie on the sand and be moderately warm; the habitués have built a number of forts on the beach, as windbreaks. Just offshore—almost reachable at low tide—is an upthrusting rock against which the waves crash, with a resounding THUD that makes the beach literally shake. On days when the surf is especially high, if you're lying down near the water, I swear you could cum just from the vibration of the sand—sort of like rubbing off on the washing machine when you were a kid. The thunder and the spray and the raw, orgasmic power of nature always makes me feel slightly drunk.

Of course I admire the men. That's a given. But if that were all I wanted, I'd go to Dolores Park instead. (And sometimes I do.) More men, lots more buffed, and it's a helluva lot easier to reach. The only difference at Land's End is that the men are naked, and if you do end up meeting someone who pushes your buttons, you can run up into the bushes and consummate the affair on the spot. (Hell, I've done it right on the beach—but that was fifteen years ago.) Somehow, this easygoing attitude fits in well with the pounding of the waves against the Rock: Two aspects of nature at her uninhibited best. A beach is all about Primal Nature, I've decided. And that's a pretty damn sexy thing.

Ripe and Ready

I am told there are some people, somewhere, who just don't like persimmons. Well, there's no accounting for taste.

Persimmons make their appearance in markets, at least on the west coast, in October. Presumably due to the limited market, they are one of the few fruits that have not yet made it into year-round availability. Reluctantly, I am forced to concede that this is a good thing. It's nice that the staples of daily life—tomatoes, lettuce, apples, and so forth—can be had year-round, but a special treat like a persimmon should be a seasonal indicator, making the autumn a time for celebration. And when I see that first batch of persimmons in the market, the associations that rush to mind are enough to make me drool.

My father would make an annual trek to southern California in September, to help his father with the autumn chores; he always brought back a box of persimmons and pomegranates from the trees in Grandad's backyard. They usually weren't ripe yet, and we'd have to wait. If you've ever tasted an unripe persimmon, you don't try it twice. We would all hover over the tray, as it sat outside, testing them daily for ripeness; when the first one was ready, it was virtually a religious rite. This is my body, this is my blood, this is my cum. Even though the color is all wrong, the consistency of persimmon pulp is just about right for cum: it's slimy, and gooey, and has an odor that cum ought to have. My mother, presumably, did not think these things; she just apportioned the pulp equally among the eager kids.

So when I see that first tray of persimmons in the market . . . my mouth starts watering in a totally unique, but totally familiar, way. I begin gulping down saliva, imagining I'm swallowing those pulpy lumps of flavor, and I grab as many as I think I can carry.

When shopping for persimmons, the primary consideration is softness. Yes, the hard ones will probably ripen, but they may require more patience than you possess. I've known them to take three months. And sometimes, if they've been picked too soon, instead of ripening they will toughen and shrivel, and you'll be left with nothing for all your anticipation. That's why it's wise to buy more than one. But it's better still if you can buy them at or near ripeness. Soft, bulging, brilliant orange-red, with clear skin: These are indicators of a good persimmon. Of course, if you get one that's really ripe, you have no chance whatsoever of getting it home with the skin intact: The slightest contact will split the skin and let the juices ooze out into the plastic bag, forcing you to turn the bag inside out and lick it clean. (Tell me you've never done this with a condom. Go on—just try to convince me.) This is, of course, the ideal way to eat a persimmon: Messily. A pox on those, like my mother, who insist on using a spoon! When I have a really ripe persimmon—one that feels like a water balloon in my hand, one that I know is bound to split of its own accord if I let it sit for just one more day—I carefully twist off the stem, I cradle it in my left hand, and then I stick my face down into it. If I've removed the stem carefully, there is a small hole that I can stick my tongue down into and start working it around, opening it up, before I begin sucking out the juices. No other dining experience comes so close to sex. The intensity of the flavor, as it hits my tongue; the sensuousness of feeling the globules sliding down my throat; the stickiness on my lips and fingers, as the skin breaks open and oozes all over the place . . . I swear, it's downright orgasmic.

(It wasn't until many years later that I learned that there is a similar secret to eating pomegranates. If you knead the hard fruit long enough, it will become pulpy and soft, like a beanbag: juiced inside the skin. Then you can bite through the skin and suck the juice out without having to deal with the seeds, trickles of red dribbling down your chin.)

The season never lasts long. There will be some fruits lingering in the markets through spring, but by that time the fascination has worn thin; they're no longer the stunning manifestation of sensuality that they were in October. I hardly notice when they disappear, having gorged myself in November and December. But then, come autumn, I find myself waiting—without quite knowing what I'm waiting for—and feeling, all over again, that rush of saliva that most of you probably associate with slurping on an especially tasty dick, when I see those harbingers of winter.

My Last Parasite

There is a pill—I've taken it before—
that drives the buggers out. It's slow, but sure.
But most folks think it's marginal improvement:
Affliction's sometimes preferable to cure.

I've lived with parasites of one form or another
nearly all my life. My parents did not choose
to have me immunized, preferring still the school
that holds protection as the proper role of mother.

I disagree; but my opinions, since I'm not a parent,
are merely hypothetical. My life,
since my majority, has been one bout of
diarrhea then another. Purges help, but only temporarily.

The doctors claim we get these beasties in our system
by doing nasty, dirty things in unclean places.
I dissent. The more that we inoculate ourselves,
the more we take our pleasures where we find 'em,

The less susceptible we are to each insidious new
infection. I have revelled in the muck and mire,
dredged each scrap of happiness, and taken my
medicinals without a qualm. It's when I try to isolate

myself, and hold myself apart, pristine—that's when
I find that I've a worm within me, siphoning my sustenance,
a worm no purgative can roust: The Parasite Within.
That's when I know it's time to eat some foreign ass.

Saturday, September 21, 1996

Feeling a Little Queer

One of the criticisms leveled at my last book (and really, folks, I'm not complaining; I like criticism, as long as it's reasonably intelligent) was that it was too morbid. "Every other page," a friend told me, "I'd be reading about another of your friends, and then you'd end the paragraph with, "but he's dead now, of course." Oh dear. I'm appalled. I hadn't even noticed this tendency (although, looking through the book, I see what he means); you see, in writing about these men, I was writing about their lives, not their deaths. Celebrating, rather than mourning. But that's just me and my rose-colored glasses again, automatically seeing just the silver lining. Nevertheless, I apologize unreservedly. I agree, it was a dreadful error. This plague should never have been allowed to get so fatal. I promise I'll never let it happen again.

Moving right along, however . . . as I've stated many times before, in *STEAM* and elsewhere, stopping the spread of AIDS is not my battle. I find it very hard to get upset about new infections. An AIDS diagnosis is far from being a death sentence nowadays; and from a purely selfish point of view, new infections are good for me. The more Diseased Pariahs there are, the larger the pool of men I consider to be "available." Besides which . . . well, the more people get infected, the more attention will be paid to finding a cure. If infections stopped tomorrow, funds—and sympathy— would dry up by Thursday. So I welcome newcomers to the club, and wish them a long and happy coexistence with the Death Spoor (as my boyfriend calls it).

Hey, don't act so shocked by my callousness. As if you hadn't had the same thoughts yourself. Everyone's well aware of this particular dynamic; it's just that no one else has been vulgar enough to put it in print. Even ACT/UPers—not generally known as models of good taste and decorum—have refrained from stating it in such crass terms. Nor are they likely to: They're very concerned with being model citizens, these days. Well, this is the section of the book where I do my best to "act up" myself, coming out with all those statements that you really wish I would keep under wraps. The ones that make the politically correct gay/lesbian/bisexual/ transgender people clear their throats nervously and look around to see if any news cameras are watching.

I don't live my life according to what "they" will think of me, or of "the gay community." I don't think anyone is liable to mistake my voice for "the voice of the gay community," and my actions are predicated on standards that are uniquely my own. I don't proselytize; I don't even assume that my standards, perspectives, and opinions would be appropriate for anyone else, much less the community at large. (How open-minded can you get?) Hanging around with gay community leaders—as is almost inevitable in San Francisco—certainly gives me a feeling of being, well, a little queer. Fortunately, I am accustomed to that.

Wholesome and Natural

Despite having had sex in a thousand public places over the years, I have never been arrested. Many of these encounters were illegal in other ways, as well: because I was in a sodomy-law state, or because I was having sex with a seventeen-year-old, or because I didn't tell my partner that I had AIDS. (In Michigan, it doesn't even matter if you tell him: PWAs just aren't allowed to have sex. I took especial delight in flouting that particular barbarism.) Sex, I kept telling my partners—usually in nonverbal terms—is nothing to be ashamed of. Sucking dick through gloryholes is not immoral or antisocial or aberrant. What's sick is the amount of energy that our society pours into trying to repress those wholesome and natural desires.

I suppose I'm preaching to the perverted, here. None of my readers is liable to be surprised by any of these declarations. But I'm continually amazed by how many gay men retain those lingering remnants of guilt and self-hatred: Men who suspect that they're "sex addicts" because they love to feel the sunlight on their backs while they're fucking someone, or because they go to dark and dirty movie theaters to watch guys get up and jack off on stage. My entire life, looking back on it, has been devoted to telling these guys: NO! You are normal—it's the society around you that's fucked up. When I have sex in Dolores Park, or at a bathhouse or sex club, or in the rest room of a public hospital (as I did recently, fulfilling a years-old fantasy) or a bookstore arcade, I do it with an intense awareness that my acts are giving the man (or men) I'm with validation for their desires.

Some people will roll their eyes and say "Yeah, sure" when they read that I was doing pornflicks to try to heal gay men's libidos. Well, there's no doubt that I was doing it for other reasons, too. I'm an exhibitionist: I like being watched. The notion that my image would be preserved forever on celluloid or videotape was an intense thrill to me. I also just liked the physical act of playing with many of my partners: Not all of them, of course, but some of those guys were lots of fun. Nevertheless . . . I have to insist that the primary motivation for me being up there in lights was to make guys feel good about themselves. When I could look out there into the audience and see men jerking off, looking up admiringly at me, I had to grin at them. These were my people: These men who were learning to be unashamed of their sexuality. I didn't just see them in the audience at the Campus Theater; I saw them at Land's End, and the Midtowne Spa, and everywhere else I "performed," whether for money or for personal satisfaction. I saw them, by proxy, in the stacks of letters I got as editor of *STEAM*: Men who wrote to thank me for the affirmation I'd given them. And they make me proud. I'm not a big booster of what has come to be called The Gay Community, but these men who I see in all these places are my community. Some are still struggling to come out, some are far less inhibited than I'll ever be, but what we share is the knowledge that sex IS wholesome and natural. It doesn't need to be hidden. It won't harm the children. It's not an assault. It's a declaration of membership in the human race.

Children are not born with a sense of shame about sex, regardless of what the hellfire-and-brimstone types would like us to believe. Children of both sexes play with their genitalia—their own and those of their playmates—freely, with no sense that it might be unacceptable to society. They don't restrict such activities to the bathroom, or under the covers; small children are just as likely to start rubbing their crotches at the dinner table or in a social gathering. And mother, shocked at this display of naturalness, will slap the little boy's hand and send him to bed without his supper. Eventually, of course, the kid gets the message: touching himself "down there" is wrong, pleasure is wrong, anything to do with his penis or asshole is dirty.

I don't even remember these lessons from my mother; they took place, I assume, before the dawn of recorded history. Being the fourth son in my family, I doubt that she was actually shocked by my behavior, but I'm sure she took draconian measures to stop it. Rather effectively, I guess: I do not recall playing with myself until

I was ten, though my curiosity about other boys' peepees began much earlier.

All these things are about as natural as you can get. I sincerely hope that in the past thirty years there has been some change in parental attitudes toward masturbation: Parents who are capable of remembering the shame and guilt visited upon them by their own parents, and who don't want to repeat the cycle. I can remember, as early as age twelve, fantasizing about how I would raise my children, to free them from the ridiculous inhibitions I'd inherited. Casual household nudity figured prominently in this fantasy; and a common sleeping area, where parents (and I didn't limit myself to two, but frequently envisioned a communal household with multiple parents; I have to give credit for this idea to Robert A. Heinlein) and children would sleep in a massive puppy-pile. This thought gave me a warm and secure feeling. Today, if put into practice, it would give me fifty-to-life.

And that's the problem, obviously. Parental attitudes may be changing, slowly, but the legal system appears to be moving in the other direction. Sexuality of all sorts, especially juvenile sexuality, is becoming more and more off-limits. The definition of what constitutes sexual harassment has gone off the deep end. I'm sure most people who heard about that seven-year-old boy who gave his classmate a kiss on the cheek thought "Oh, how sweet." A century ago, fifty years ago, even ten years ago, I think that would have been the reaction. Now, thanks to this new version of politically correct puritanism, any expression of affection is considered taboo, because it might lead to sex. We would be a healthier society if we could get over this phobia of touching, of affection—of sex.

I suppose I should be grateful to my parents. You see, they didn't tell me that hugging or kissing was bad; they just made it clear, by their own behavior, that it Wasn't Done. I never saw any affection between them; I don't believe either of them ever touched me, except in the most utilitarian way. Holding my hand when we crossed the street, that sort of thing. So on that incredible afternoon—April 16, 1977—when a man said to this trembling, shaking adolescent, "Let me hold you," the world burst into fireworks and flowers, and I didn't have the slightest doubt that what we were doing was right and wonderful. I did not have any sense of it being "immoral" or "unnatural"; it was the most natural thing in the world, the thing I'd been waiting for all my life. I cried. I cried for the years that I'd wasted in isolation, and the more years that I knew would pass before I could really join the human race. And possibly, just a little, I cried for my parents, who I somehow knew had never experienced anything like this. How could they? The only person they'd publicly admit to loving was Jesus.

Years went by. I knew, of course, that sex was not "supposed" to be a public act, but I don't recall ever having any doubts about its essential rightness. I knew, with a confidence that came from somewhere Other, that my parents were Wrong: Deeply, intrinsically wrong. Not evil, but misled. Sex was good; sharing my body with another person was an affirmation of everything positive in life, and making a public display of that sexuality was one of the most basic ways in which I could improve the world. So I had sex in all the places where we're not supposed to do it: Parks, beaches, bathhouses, bars, back alleys. Did I feel fear? You bet. It was clear to me, at even the tenderest age, that there were evil men in uniform out there who were devoted to the suppression of sex, and the thought of being in the grip of this gestapo was one of the most frightening things I could imagine. These are the ones I call the antilife patrol, the ones who, instead of intimacy and affection, merely crave control over other people. They are, and always have been, the enemy. They've arrested the producers of the films I've been in; they've arrested a friend of mine who had a mutually rewarding relationship with a child, with the approval of the child's parents; they would like to prevent magazines like *STEAM* from being published. They have good reason to be afraid of sex: Once people discover the potential for pleasure in their bodies, I think they become a lot less willing to submit to external authority.

It's my unwillingness to accept that authority at face value that has made me an effective "Pleasure Activist" (thank you, Annie Sprinkle)—and, at times, a lightning rod for criticism. I've come out in favor of sex on film, public sex, anonymous sex, intergenerational sex, Positive sex, and "unsafe" sex; in each case, I've raised someone's hackles. The bottom line is that I believe that sex is inherently good. The nice thing about the gay community, insofar as it exists, is that there has been some effort to accept sex as an integral part of life. The gay men I know are not ashamed of their sex lives. When my friends go out to a sex club, I'll probably get a call the next day, with a vivid report of what went on. This casual attitude toward sex—this unwillingness to lie about, hide, or disguise our sexual cravings—is one of the primary "bonds" of my community.

My only regret is that this group of men is still not being given the chance to pass on these values to the next generation. I know they could do a helluva lot better job than my parents did.

Ah, Unity

"We don't want you in our parade!" "You deserve to die!"
"You're not part of the gay community!" These were some of the
lovely things shouted at us—through a bullhorn, appropriately
enough—by a couple of lesbian "comedians" on a flatbed truck in
one of the San Francisco Gay Day parades. I don't remember which
year; I marched in seven of them, always with the same group.
Invariably, along the route, we would get a steady rain of hisses,
jeers, and insults from people along the route (together with a
smaller amount of cheering). I was used to that. Mostly, this abuse
came from women, but a few men joined in. Peer pressure, you
know. Political correctness. But these dykes on the float ahead of us
... this was really a bit much. I don't remember their names, but the
float was sponsored by the Eureka Theater Company. After the
parade, I sent a letter of protest to the Eureka; I got back a letter
saying that they supported the position taken by their spokespeople.

Later that year, the Eureka experienced economic woes; I have
seldom been happy to see a theater company go financially bank-
rupt, but in this case it seemed to match their moral condition.

You'll probably have guessed by now what contingent I was
marching with. Yes, the North American Man/Boy Love Association: NAMBLA. That first year, 1984, when I showed up at the
staging area for the parade, I don't think I had any definite ideas of
who I'd be marching with; there were half a dozen possibilities.
Different Spokes, the gay Libertarians, the bowling league, or
maybe one of the clubs' floats ... I was sure I'd find something. I
got there, and saw NAMBLA, and knew that was the place for me.
Because I like boys? Not hardly. I've never been comfortable
around children, much less sexually attracted to them. I've always
preferred older men: Men with some experience, men who can
teach me, men who are secure and self-confident and responsible.
And I'm no longer a boy, so no, technically speaking, I can't be a

NAMBLA member. But I realized right away that this was the most stigmatized, the most loathed, group in the parade . . . and that was where I belonged.

I kept it up for the next six years; every year, it was a lesson in just how sincere the term "gay community" really is. Every year, we were reviled and harassed. I don't think we were ever physically attacked, but it was close. And I confess, I never understood the hatred we inspired. These were people with permanently closed minds, slammed shut like a prison door. They had no interest whatsoever in hearing anything that contradicted their doctrine. Sounds a lot like some fundamentalist preachers I could name.

Now, I know I've talked about my own childhood at length, but maybe it can bear repeating one more time, in brief. I started having sex with men when I was fifteen, and I thought I was a ridiculously late bloomer. I'd been fantasizing about it, wishing for it, since I was twelve—and those three years were the longest of my life. If what Douglas did to me was "molestation," I'm a pie-eyed greebus. And the men I knew who were members of NAMBLA were certainly not interested in forcing themselves on children; they were involved in mutually loving, supportive, playful, and wholesome relationships with boys who might otherwise have had to go without. I wish I had met someone like that when I was twelve—or ten, or eight, for that matter.

Getting down to brass tacks: no, I do not believe there is any age at which it is inherently wrong for a child to be sexually active. What is wrong is coercion, of any sort. But I do know enough about children to know that when they don't want to do something, they're not afraid to say so. I also know that there is not a single NAMBLA member who would not be outraged at the thought of forcing a child—or anyone—to have sex. The only issue, really, is whether a child of ten is capable of giving "consent." I say he is, if his parents have given him any responsibility at all. Establishing a special category for children—or for gays, or ethnic minorities, or women, or the disabled—and giving them special "protection" merely enshrines their disadvantaged status, gives the authorities more power, and ensures that the dynamics will never change. Basic Libertarian Theory 101, here: government "protection" is the first step on the road to the concentration camps.

Eventually, the protests in San Francisco and other cities grew so loud that the various parade committees refused to allow NAMBLA to march anymore. That's when I quit going in disgust. No, I'd never felt very much a part of these dreary political extravaganzas, but this just made it blatantly obvious that they were no longer interested in any pretense of tolerance. It was now a closed shop, with privileges for a select few.

Ironically, the same year that NAMBLA got banned from several parades, a group of gay Irishmen sued the Saint Patrick's Day Parade in New York City to be allowed to march with them. The irony was completely lost on the parade organizers.

Let me backtrack a bit. All those people lining the parade routes, spitting vitriol at us, were determined that we were "child molesters." Let me tell you about the one time I definitely *was* molested. I don't actually remember it, but I was strapped down and a part of me—a useful, functioning part, no different from a finger or an ear—was cut off. Yeah, that's right: my foreskin. I will proclaim from the rooftops: my parents were child molesters. I am occasionally tempted to file a civil suit against them for infliction of emotional distress—not for money, but in hopes that it might cause more parents to stop and think before authorizing that mutilation. But no, I can't handle the stress of a court fight, I'm afraid, and I don't want to have to deal with them.

But I do dream about the day, sometime in the future, when there is a massive "war crimes" tribunal set up to prosecute the doctors who perform and condone this monstrous practice. This is real child abuse, practiced daily in every hospital in the country . . . and do these lesbians who hiss at NAMBLA have anything to say about it? Nada. This shows me just how concerned they really are with the children. No, they're just like our parents: They just want to retain control over us. They resent the fact that children grow up, and become independent. Seems odd, to me, that women who identify as lesbians should be so territorial about children . . . but there are lots of things I don't understand.

Let me shift gears, here: I have a friend who describes himself as a socialist. (Well, probably more than one, but one in particular.) He and I see eye to eye on very few issues. And that's just fine, because we are both rational individuals, capable of disagreeing in civil tones, without letting the conversation degenerate into a spitting catfight. I respect him—and I rather think he respects me—because I know that his philosophy, divergent from my own though it may be, is the product of logical thought. He hasn't just picked his opinions off the nearest party line doctrine-tree. He's given serious consideration to each of them. And that's the difference between him and the hissing hordes: They've picked up their opinions, ready-made, because that's what everyone else thinks. And frankly, I can't imagine anything more actively evil than that. Being willing to give up your capacity for skepticism, just so that you will have a group to disappear in, another group to despise . . . ugh.

I guess that's why the numbers quoted for the parades fail to impress me very much. Yeah, sure, a hundred thousand, two hundred thousand—what's the difference? They're all trying to blend into one group mind. I think I get more stimulation, more support, more encouragement, out of an evening sitting and talking with a group of six widely divergent individuals, each with his own strongly held beliefs, than I will ever get from the teeming hordes and huddled masses with but one thought between them: The intense desire not to be alone. To be united.

Is That a Tumor on Your Tummy,
or . . . ?

I lay on the padded table, face down, butt up, waiting. I didn't wait long: I heard someone come into the room; I heard the familiar snap of rubber; I felt a hand massaging my butthole, as I tried to relax. I didn't want to look, just yet, to see who it was.

After just a few seconds, the hand went away, and I heard that sound of rubber again. "You can get up now," he said. "I'm Dr. Anwar."

I couldn't keep from smiling at the sudden flashback. Yes, there were lots of times in my life when I lay on a padded bench, waiting . . . and often got poked and prodded by men whose faces I didn't see until afterward, if ever; men whose names I may never have learned at all. Okay, a visit to the proctologist doesn't quite take the place of a night at the Steamworks, in my erotic repertoire, but the resemblance is remarkable. I've been down there five times in the past five months (these warts are persistent), and I've been seen (and poked and prodded) by five different doctors. Most of them were in and out of the room inside a minute; none of them were particularly memorable. That is, until I looked up and saw Dr. Anwar, and realized that here was a man I wouldn't mind encountering under similar-but-different circumstances. Not that I'm likely to, of course. I suspect that my days (nights) of lying face down on a mattress at the baths, open to the passing parade, are gone for good. And the doctor was nothing if not professional with me— though if there's one thing I've learned about doctors, in my (unfortunately) extensive interactions with them, it's that you shouldn't make assumptions. Once out of the lab coat, they can undergo a remarkable transformation.

It was about four years ago that I first began to realize the erotic potential of hospitals. That was the time when I started spending entirely too much time in waiting rooms, and usually, the waiting rooms were filled with other guys who were Positive. That's always a turn-on for me. A lot of them were fairly emaciated. Well, I didn't start out with a fetish for skeletons, but after a few weeks or months, I began to see the advantages of playing with someone who didn't crush me when he rolled over on top of me. I was also pretty sure that most of these guys would have a reduced energy level/libido that wouldn't overwhelm my own—a common problem when I'm trying to play with one of those disgustingly healthy gym-bunnies. But—well, okay, what it really came down to was the recognition that these were men with whom I had something in common. Something rather important. And I'd begun to feel that I didn't share much, anymore, with the Negative gay community.

I've mostly gotten over this feeling of alienation, but the attraction to Positives, and to men in hospital waiting rooms, and yes, the doctors and technicians themselves, remains. I eagerly look forward to each doctor's appointment, and I don't object in the least if I'm kept waiting. Blood draws are no longer an ordeal . . . at least, as long as Senor Flores is the one doing the draw. I just spend the time looking at his eyebrows. No, I have never gone home with any of these guys. The cruising, if you can call it that, has been limited to that specific environment. (I was, on one occasion, persuaded to join a fellow patient in a rest room; the sex was quick and satisfying, his cum was quite tasty, and the rest of the day I could hardly keep from grinning whenever I thought about it. But I digress.) I'm almost afraid to try. It's not even cruising that's going on there, so much as camaraderie, an unspoken acknowledgement of a common acceptance and celebration. (I have this mental image of the lot of us doing a chorus line, singing, "We are the Positive Conspiracy/ Sex is our favorite heresy!" Not ready for Broadway, huh? Okay.) I look into their eyes and smile, and the message that passes is so much more explicit (and amusing) than what you experience under other circumstances. It's probably something like, "Yeah, I'd love to go home with you, but I've got an infusion this afternoon, so I know I'm gonna feel like shit for the rest of the day . . . and besides, I've got this diarrhea . . . " Not the sexiest of messages, huh? Well . . . there was a time when I wouldn't have thought so, either. But you've gotta admit: it's real.

Just to reassure you all somewhat: No, I don't find all hospital visits exciting. That barium enema I had last month was one of the more unpleasant things that's ever happened to me; even the novelty of being able to look at my colon on a video monitor didn't do anything for me (though I probably should have asked them for a videotape, to sell to all my truly obsessive fans). X rays don't particularly turn me on—though there was that memorable one, years ago, when the technician was wondering aloud what "that shadow" stretching across my lower belly, all the way up to my navel, could be. I assured her that it was nothing abnormal, or at least nothing to worry about. And of course I have encountered my share of Doctors From Hell, docs who don't know, don't care, and don't particularly want to answer questions. Somehow, I manage to keep my sense of humor intact through even the worst of them . . . and then occasionally, I encounter someone like Dr. Anwar, and allow myself the distinct pleasure of thinking that, even if I never encounter him at the baths, I did at least have his finger up my butt once. This is not a fantasy; it's reality.

Medicine is a funny field. It's all about the body (well, if you exclude psychiatry for the moment), but doctors themselves are not supposed to even *have* bodies. A friend of mine tells of the time in med school when they were learning how to do procto exams; he was paired up with the most prudish guy in the class. So Mark made sure that his butt was all loosened up beforehand, and when the other guy tentatively started to probe with his finger, Mark did his Asshole-That-Ate-Cincinnati number, and swallowed the guy's whole hand. Well, that's what he told me. Makes a good story, and a good fantasy. Freaked the poor boy out, of course. Now, Mark was perfectly capable, I know, of swallowing almost anything that touched his asshole—the hunger of that hole is rivaled, in my experience, only by Chris Burns—but that didn't mean that I had any desire to see him dressed in a surgical gown while he was doing me. I'm afraid that would only have made me laugh. And most guys take offense when you can't take their fantasies seriously.

There was a time when my sex life was ruled by Fantasy. All my sex partners were the biggest, the best, the raunchiest, the prettiest, the kinkiest, the ultimate. Well, okay, not all of them; relatively few, in fact. But those were the ones that stood out, the ones I gushed about in my journal, the ones I dreamed about and jerked off over for weeks afterward: The Gods of Sex. Some of these encounters were recorded on video, Reality transmuted to Fantasy: My Reality, the audience's Fantasy. I'm glad that they're out there, permanently available as a reminder of what I was like at age twenty-two, but I seldom watch them anymore. Mine, or anyone else's. In the intervening years, I think I've come to prefer Reality to Fantasy . . . and somewhat unintentionally, a hospital has come to be a major part of my Reality. I don't suppose it's any surprise that I should have come to eroticize these visits. The men I see there are Real—god, are they ever. Reality has hit them over the head in a big way, and most of them have given up the competition to be Mr. Fantasy. I've *been* Mr. Fantasy, thank you; it was nice, in a way, but now it's over, and I'm inclined to say that this is a good thing.

Some of you will probably remember a video called *In Your Wildest Dreams,* in which, yes, I did play a doctor's assistant. Falcon likes these fantasy scenarios. The doctor and I stuffed all the usual things up our "patient's" butt—dicks, fists, dildos—although I don't think it was ever explained just what the patient's problem was. Maybe we were trying to find a tumor? Obviously, I'm suffering from an excess of Reality (or you can call it cynicism, if you prefer), but this setup struck me as absurd, rather than erotic. Today, what would be my reaction if Dr. Anwar had started probing more deeply—and then maybe called in Sr. Flores to help him? Well, it makes a nice fantasy, but it wasn't really what I wanted. Trying to bring a fantasy into the realm of Reality usually ends up killing it. I'd rather have plain, ordinary, everyday Reality. It's seldom as exotic, but in the long run it tends to be more satisfying.

"And what's your viral load?" Hey, it's better than "What's your sign?"

The Opinionated Pervert

It is election day, and I will shortly be going to the polls. Not that there's anything of great significance on the ballot this year—a few dull propositions, only one of which has aroused any controversy. No need for me to go into it; the issue itself is unimportant. But I'm going to the polls to register my ongoing dissatisfaction with government in general. As I said to a friend last night, who asked me which way I was voting on this particular proposition, "I vote against, on principle."

I vote against, because any ballot initiative is designed to do one of two things: Squeeze more money out of the taxpayers, or coerce someone into doing something. Once in a blue moon, there will be an initiative on the ballot that is written to force politicians to do something they don't want to do—generally, give up some of their power—and those, I will vote for. They're usually targeted at specific legislation that the politicians have passed, as a way of letting them know that this time they've gone too far. These initiatives are never very effective, since politicians are always a step ahead of the initiative-writers, and have already figured out a way to get around the limitations on their power; but sometimes they do slow down the growth of big government.

If all of this sounds excessively cynical, I can only claim experience. There is a struggle going on in the world, as Billy Graham likes to remind us; he and I differ, however, on who the combatants are. I maintain that the struggle is between those who want to control human behavior and those who would rather let people control themselves. The former camp is made up primarily of people who lack a moral sense, and therefore assume that everyone else is similarly handicapped, and needs to be monitored continuously: Our driving habits, our eating, drinking, and recreational pleasures—and especially anything to do with sex—should all be subject to their approval and regulation. Treated like children, in other words. And then there are the libertarians among us, who believe that man, left to his own devices, will develop a code of conduct which is beneficial both for himself and for society. And they call *us* cynics.

Expounding this view to my friend last night, however, made me consider what exceptions I've made to this "Rule of No." I could only come up with one: The Medical Marijuana Initiative—another classic example of a voter referendum whose major effect has been to give the politicians a chance to display their piety and puritanism in the face of a hedonistic populace. It's been a very long time since I voted yes on anything else. Yes, I would have voted for the famous property tax limitation imposed by California voters all those years ago, if I'd been a California resident at the time, but I would have done so with the foregone conclusion that it wouldn't do any real good. (And I don't think it has.) Another example came to mind immediately: Amendment 2, in Colorado, which prohibited local governments from passing "gay rights" laws. Believe it or not, this is a borderline issue for me. Yes, I'm sure that many of the backers of the amendment were motivated by small-mindedness and bigotry, but that doesn't change the fact that this was an initiative designed to curtail the power of government, rather than extend it. And you know, frankly, I think that anyone who relies on governmental fiat to change society is the same sort of person who is in danger of mistaking *Fantasia* for a documentary on dinosaurs. People don't change just because politicians pass a law mandating it. People change when they understand that it is in their best interest to change; when they see the tangible benefits of change.

The ultimate argument of those who accuse me of idealism—an accusation I don't wish to dispute—is that in the process of waiting for "market forces" to work, I would sacrifice hundreds, even thousands, of lives. Legislation, they say, is the only way to protect those helpless gay people (insert: people of color, women, disabled, whatever) from the prejudice and hatred they may encounter in the world. They're right; I don't believe in "protecting" anyone from hatred. Nor do I wish to be protected. The problem with such protection, aside from the fact that it doesn't work, is that it institutionalizes the division: It makes both hater and hated assume the conflict as a given—and, not coincidentally, gives the mediator/

bureaucrat a cast-iron, rock-solid, permanent job. The primary job of any bureaucrat is to perpetuate his own job; a really successful bureaucrat is one who manages to enlarge the problem to the extent that he ends up needing seventeen minions. From that perspective, I would say that the government department that administers "Civil Rights" laws has been phenomenally successful, but as far as eliminating prejudice and discrimination . . . well, remember that Nordic king who stood on the beach and commanded the waves to stop?

Which brings us back to that confusing Amendment 2. I still don't know how I would have voted on it; I think it would have depended on the precise wording, which I don't recall. If it included any language that sounded even vaguely religious or moralistic, or referred specifically to "the homosexual lifestyle," I couldn't have supported it, but if it were drawn narrowly enough, merely prohibiting local governments from giving one group preference over another—and if it included other "minority protection laws" under its prohibition—why yes, that's something I could endorse wholeheartedly.

Of course, the Supreme Court's ruling that it was unconstitutional may have something to do with this attitude. It's that old rebellious streak, you know: I have difficulty accepting the supremes' rulings as gospel. And ever since the Hardwick case, I've generally taken anything they say with about a ton of salt. Now there's a case on which I have no uncertainty at all: It was government intrusion into private lives, at its very worst. I think even my father would have a hard time disagreeing with me on that . . . though he would also have a hard time admitting that he agreed with me on anything.

Okay, so now that I've ingratiated myself to all those Democratic Party types who think that government is the solution to everything (do I really have any such people among my readership? I suppose it's possible. Hey, people buy my books for the literary equivalent of a one-night stand—and I've been known to make remarkable concessions, politically and philosophically, when my politics interfere with getting laid)—I'd like to do the Texas Two-Step around the issue and equivocate a bit. Just because I'm a Libertarian (both small-l and capital-L, thank you) doesn't mean that my opinions are cast in concrete. I love listening to other opinions, debating them, hearing perspectives that I may not have experienced personally.

Most of my friends disagree with me, politically, and that's just fine with me. (If I limited myself to knowing only other Libertarians, I'd have a very small social circle.) My only requirement is that they not be the foaming-at-the-mouth types, the ones who believe in the biblical injunction of "You are either for me or against me." Discussion is not the same as argument. I don't expect to change anyone else's mind (hell, I think I'd respect them less if I were able to: I like a person who has already given thorough consideration to his opinions, and who may modify them, over time, but is unsusceptible to sudden conversions), and I am unlikely to change my own, at least in any radical way, but debate is still a healthy thing— sharpens the mind, don't you know.

Oddly enough, that's my major complaint with writing as a profession: No feedback. No debate. Oh, there is some, of course; mostly, it comes from reviewers, who feel free to skewer the writer with their wit (or lack thereof), secure in the knowledge that there's no opportunity for rebuttal. I am grateful for what useful advice they offer. But that's hardly a healthy parry and riposte. Editors, I have concluded, are a good thing (contrary to what many writers think) precisely because they are able to spot many of the discrepancies and ambiguities that would otherwise be candy for the more merciless critics. Still, nothing is quite as stimulating as a lively sparring session with a deeply committed Socialist—if one can be found who is willing to lower his standards far enough to debate issues with a Libertarian. Occasionally I worry, in my wilder flights of fancy, about what would happen if the world ever did adopt a truly individualist perspective on life. Life would be awfully boring without all those collectivists doing their collective thing. Fortunately, there is little chance of this ever happening. . . .

And now I must gird my loins and go into the voting booth. Girding the loins, for some strange reason, is required before going out in public. I look forward to the day when I can vote for an initiative to repeal *that* curious relic of Victorianism.

Kilo-Mania

There was a video that some of you may recall—*Sighs*, directed by Ron Pearson—in which I had to pretend to be a gym queen. The camera lovingly pans over me as I lie there bench pressing, with my dick hanging out of my shorts. Now, I'd researched the role: I'd actually signed up at that gym for a one-month trial membership several weeks earlier, so I'd have some familiarity with the machines. Pointless. Watching that video, today, is extremely embarrassing. Some people's physiques just aren't meant to be seen on weight benches.

Mind you, once I got into the Jacuzzi with Joel Curry, I felt no such alienation. This was my element.

I've never felt the urge to "work out." Without trying to be judgmental about it, there are better ways of spending my life than repeatedly lifting the same pieces of metal. When I lived in Wisconsin, I built rock walls: Over the course of three years, I probably lifted as much weight as your average gym queen does in the same period, and every day I could look out the window and see the progress. I turned an overgrown hillside into a terraced, landscaped rock garden. Taught me something about the importance (to me, anyway) of visual evidence of my accomplishments. Did some nice things for my shoulders, too.

But that's all in the past. These days, the most exercise I get is some bicycling and walking. Lots of walking. Good for me, but my shoulders have faded back to obscurity. And whenever I happen to be in the GI department of the hospital, the dietician always corners me. Grills me about my eating habits, and then starts in on his pet obsession: The importance of resistance exercise, to build lean muscle mass. I've learned not to say anything. Any response only makes him go on longer.

There was a time—quite a few years ago, now—when I felt insecure about my body. I was the ninety-seven-pound weakling that all those physical training companies who advertise in the back of boys' magazines make a mint off of. Not that I ever ordered one of their products; I just jerked off over their brochures. Eventually I realized that my body was just fine, thanks, without any augmentation. (Being hired to do jack-off shows did wonders for my self-esteem. Who needs twenty-inch biceps?) Over the years, I've laughed at the pressures in gay society to join a gym. I suppose I can understand the appeal of hanging out in the company of all those other buff guys—hey, I like to look at them as much as the next queerboy—but somehow it doesn't seem worth the membership fees, not to mention the time spent in nonproductive repetitive motion. And yeah, it saddens me to see so many gay men still operating under the low self-esteem engendered by those adolescent images of Charles Atlas. Really, guys, I feel like saying: Isn't there something better you could be doing with your lives?

That's why I get especially burned up when I hear the same drivel thrown at me from my medical providers. Mark is an excessively "nice" person, and I'm sure he's concerned with nothing but my health, and I still want to throttle him every time he starts off on his spiel. He's certainly teaching me a thing or two about resistance: I'm feeling extremely resistant to most anything he says, these days. Would exercise be "good for me?" No, I'm sorry, but I won't even concede that. It would build muscle, and stamina, and it would bore me to tears. And I would probably end up by snapping: buying an Uzi and slaughtering the entire herd of beef.

Since 90 percent of you are probably devoted to your hours at the gym, I've lost most of my audience already. "It's a social outlet!" I hear you scream, and so it is. As such, it's a 100 percent improvement over bars. And really, I'm not trying to deny anyone their pleasures. I just wish that there weren't quite so much pressure to conform to the social expectations. Muscle either is built to perform a function, or it's redundant. There is no need for a librarian to look like Arnold. But somehow, in the process of building a sense of gay pride, we've all accepted the image of the buff bodybuilder as the ideal.

Codeine Is God

To paraphrase someone or other, "Some are born naive; others have naivete thrust upon 'em." (For all its alliterative appeal, I don't think it's quite semantically possible to "achieve naivete.") I tend to think that I was one of the latter group. When you originate in an area where you are, arguably, one of the more "sophisticated" persons around, and then relocate to a much more jaded environment, you suddenly become, ipso facto, naive.

(For those who would question how one achieves sophistication in isolation, I respond: This is the Communication Age. There is no such thing as true Isolation.)

In my youth (said the sage, as he shook his grey locks), I knew very little about pharmaceuticals, whether prescribed or proscribed. My family shunned both types, for different reasons. At the age when my education in such matters commenced, I was under the tutelage of a rather experienced woman, who seemed to know the name and purpose of every pill ever manufactured. She had a lot of them in her medicine cabinet. I began to feel how naive I was in such matters. She introduced such words as "blotter" and "windowpane" into my vocabulary (not to mention the poets who had used them), and at one point, she brought up the subject of codeine, with reverence in her voice. I heard, but did not understand; I was young enough that I was not yet interested in mere painkillers. As I expressed it, in my snotty youth, "I don't want to take drugs that just make me feel 'okay.' I want drugs that make me feel *fabulous!*" I can't say that my wish was fulfilled very many times over the years. My education proceeded by leaps and bounds and great soaring flights of hallucination; my life was not significantly improved thereby, but I survived the drop, for which I'm grateful. And here I am, trying to set out some signposts for a generation that doesn't (ever, ever, ever) want them.

It's not that I'm opposed to recreational drugs. Far from it. They have their purposes, and I'm very happy that I experienced them.

They facilitated my maturation . . . but more through what they didn't give me than through what they gave me. They didn't give me wisdom or enlightenment, or pleasure, or release from my worries. Drugs, they say, don't give you anything new; they just intensify what's already there. They certainly did that: they made me aware of a lot that was churning inside me, that needed to come out. My life (and one MGB convertible) was turned upside down. No complaints; everyone ought to have the opportunity to have their lives shaken up every now and then. Thank goodness I survived— and all I have to do now is watch. Watching someone else "have a good time" is quite exhausting enough for me, thank you.

Meanwhile, back on the other side of the legal fence . . . I was gradually approaching the age when I was interested in little else, as Richard Howard put it, but "a school where we learn how to die." (That makes me sound absolutely decrepit. All I can say is that I think the invention of AIDS, in the spirit of this Age of Convenience, has speeded up the process somewhat. There was a time when this school might have required a fifty-year matriculation. We now have the extremely popular "Death for Tourists" course: From disco to death knell in three months flat, sometimes. What will they think of next?) I began learning more about the drugs that make one feel "okay." Acyclovir was the first. I felt like I was making a pact with the devil: "As long as you take one of these pills a day *for the rest of your life,* you'll never have another of those incredibly painful sores again. Sign here, please." The absence of pain began to seem like a reasonable facsimile of pleasure. This is the first step in dying.

Later came many others, of varying effectiveness. Antibiotics, steroids, antifungals, hormones, antiretrovirals, prophylactics of the chemical kind . . . gradually my medicine cabinet came to resemble those of that "older generation," those collections of pills that so awed (yet appalled) me when I was too vigorous to ever need anything more than an aspirin. Aspirin I now disdained; there were more sophisticated painkillers.

It was in the arena of the painkillers that I discovered the most charming symbiosis between the two groups of drugs. How amusing to watch, for instance, as the Baby Boomers (who popularized a drug as Recreational in the sixties), as they aged and became more concerned with such things as aching joints and glaucoma, began voting to make it a medical treatment (again as it has been for thousands of years). I was born at the tail end of the Boom, and allow myself the grim pleasure of watching them go through, with massive nationwide publicity, the same agonies which I know I will undergo in a few years. (They'll say, "Tough shit, kid." This is what older siblings always say.) And so I learned about Roxicet and hydroxyzine, ibuprofen, tolmetin and cyclobenzaprine. These are the drugs—well, yes, I hate to say it, but *these* are the drugs—that have "improved" my life. And then, after more than a decade of absence, my life was really changed by a wonder drug. Codeine.

There are times when life is not worth living, when you have to force yourself, daily, to go on through the day rather than putting a plastic bag over your head. When the pain is so bad that all you can do is lie on the floor moaning for it to go away, and all the ibuprofen in the world can't touch it, but only makes you vomit on the floor. It was at one of these nadirs that I discovered the powers of the opium poppy. Now, I know that there are probably millions of people who are addicted to morphine and its derivatives; I realize that there are thousands of lives destroyed annually by it. What aspect of modern life, I ask you, can escape such accusations? Television is a far worse drug, in my opinion: More of a bomb and less of a balm. There was a period of a month when I took a codeine pill every day, allowing me the blessed relief to let me accomplish (some of) my daily duties, allowing me to sit up, to read, to sleep . . . and to realize that yes, life might still be worth living. Eventually, the underlying problem was diagnosed and treated. But would I have been able to hold out as long as I did, without those reminders of what life without pain can be like? I doubt it.

One of the side effects of living in San Francisco and having AIDS is that doctors are a bit more sympathetic to such distress. I am now able to keep a constant supply of this wonder drug by my bedside, as ready as the glass of water and the phone. I have used exactly two of them in the past year. They don't even tempt me, as a recreational drug; after all, they just make me feel . . . okay. Pleasantly spacey, contented without being disoriented (unlike marijuana, which usually makes me feel quite out of control). If there is pain, it no longer matters. I can think again. And that's what I miss most, when I'm in real pain: Thought. When pain fills my whole body and mind with that pulsing red wave, I can think of nothing but the pain, and pleas to someone, anyone, to make it GO AWAY! I do not believe in god, whether christian or any other variety, but at those moments, I talk to the gods. Any gods. And the only god that has ever answered has been a chemical one.

I think the analogy is realistic. After all, I don't ask codeine to take care of my occasional toothaches; I go to the dentist. I doubt that most religious people ask for supernatural help in cleaning their refrigerators, either, even though it may be a truly frightening prospect. No, you save your deities for the times when you are pushed absolutely to the wall. Would twelve-steppers be horrified or indulgent of my idea of making my "Higher Power" a chemical? I have no idea, and no interest in asking them. But having that bottle by my bedside, however infrequently I use it, gives me the reassurance that life can go on.

In Recovery

It is with wry amusement that I feel called upon to write a rebuttal to my own argument, written just a few months ago, in favor of drugs. I mean, wouldn't it be easier to just forget I ever wrote that piece, to quietly drop it in the trash can? Perhaps, but I can't do that. Because all the things I said in it are still true; there have been changes in my perspective, but I don't think the world has actually changed. And I don't want to just avoid the subject altogether, either: It remains an important one to me, and one that causes me a lot of confusion. Better to put all that down on paper. When I'm confused, I usually prefer to say so.

So . . . I've spent the past six months learning a lot about drugs. Recreational drugs, drugs that do destroy lives; the sort of drugs with which, I realize, I had never had more than a passing acquaintance before. Speed, especially: Methamphetamine. Nasty stuff, most everyone agrees. A real life wrecker. And it has wrecked thousands of lives, all around me, for the past two decades—and I've been blithely oblivious, because that's the way I am. I take people at face value, and one of the most basic characteristics of a speed freak, I've learned, is that he will never tell the truth, especially about himself. I learned all this the hard way—well, one of the hard ways: By being in love with an addict.

I'm still in love with him, and I'm happy to say that he's been clean these past six months. And so have I, although it was not the struggle for me that it has been for him. Giving up alcohol has caused me the occasional twinge of regret; for instance, when I'm having sushi, I miss being able to drink sake with it. And these occasional moments serve as useful reminders of what he's going through, every moment of every day. They remind me to be more tolerant than I might otherwise be.

None of this means that my feelings about codeine have changed. I still keep that bottle by my bedside. But it's been eight months since I've needed one, and I've become extremely sensitive to the thought that I might be using them "recreationally." I was tempted, a couple of months ago: I had a phone interview scheduled, and I was nervous about it. I knew a codeine would calm my nerves, make me relaxed and mellow and more coherent. And suddenly I recognized the sort of rationalization that all drug addicts go through when they use, and I was, frankly, ashamed. There is a very distinct line between "using" and "abusing"; it may not be the same for everyone, but you know it when you approach it. (After you cross it, most people are very good at losing sight of it.) I didn't want to go there. And I didn't. I know I gave a perfectly dreadful interview, but at least I was sober.

I was right, of course, in my supposition that twelve-steppers would frown on the use of a drug as my "Higher Power." Mind you, they don't prescribe what your HP ought to be, but I think the use of a drug would absolutely mortify most of them. Okay, I've adopted another HP, one that's a little less tangible, one that's a bit more vague in concept: Something that I used to think of merely as the Moral Sense. It's not an animate personality, but merely a fact of life: If you Live Well, if you do the things that your conscience tells you to do, things will go well with you. Typically Pollyanna of me, but also very pragmatic and very experience-based. This is how my life has always been. It's the times when I forget about that Moral Sense that get me into trouble, psychically. It doesn't have much to do with morals, in the sense that most people use the word; monogamy and "decency" are concepts completely foreign to me, and that's what my parents were mostly thinking of when they talked about "the moral life." But it does include a sense of respect for other people, an absolute acceptance of responsibility for my own actions, and a tendency to assume that others are acting out of similar goodwill. None of which conflict with the appropriate use of codeine, or any other necessary drug, to alleviate occasional pain.

Occasional pain. That's what the difference comes down to, I think. My life, taken as a whole, has been about 95 percent pleasure and 5 percent pain; many of the people whose stories I've listened to in the program seem to have led lives that sound rather like nightmares to me. It's no mystery why they abused drugs; I probably would, too, if my life were as miserable as all that. Drugs, of whatever sort, acted as an anesthetic, or at least a distraction, from the dismal reality of life. And then, after a while, I suppose they just got into the habit of using, and didn't know how to stop. Recovery is the process of, first, breaking that habit, and second (and most important) doing something about those things that were making life unbearable.

There are some obvious differences between my life and the average addict's life. But there is one essential similarity: Recreational drugs never did anything to improve it. Sometimes they were annoying, sometimes disastrous; sometimes they really made me wretched. I kept on trying them—occasionally—thinking, "maybe this time it'll be different." It never was. Bottom line: I'm having too much fun in this life, and I don't want to miss a minute of it. Drugs diminish my capacity, make my faculties untrustworthy, make me forget the very real, wonderful experiences I had while zonked. And I didn't much enjoy being around people who were similarly diminished. I prefer this new group: People who are actively working to improve their lives, to figure out ways of making the world a better place. All very noble and altruistic of me, what?

And then again . . . well, there are a helluva lot of real cute men at these meetings.

Going Through a Phase

There are good reasons why I live in San Francisco at present. I have to keep reminding myself of them, however, every time I see a meter minion issuing tickets for cars that don't have their wheels properly curbed or motorcycles parked on the sidewalk; every time I read about the latest expression of lesbian/gay/bisexual/transgender lunacy from our Totally Inclusive Friends at City Hall; every time I wait half an hour for The Bus That Never Came; and most recently, when I walked down into the Castro—really, generally considered to be a friendly, welcoming sort of place—and saw a flyer tacked up on a lightpost: a notice to straight people that they were trespassing on "our" territory, they were not welcome, and they'd better refrain from any overt displays of affection while they were our "guests."

Now, admittedly, this broadside was written in such virulent terms that it seemed more like a parody of itself than a reality, but alas, it's all too clear from recent events that there are a number of people who feel that way. I feel pity, and more than a little disgust, for the sort of person who feels threatened by seeing a man and a woman holding hands, or pushing a baby carriage (both examples were used in the flyer as "breeder behavior" that was unacceptable). The Castro, to me, is not about being gay. What it does symbolize for me is the freedom to be who you feel comfortable being; to do what you want to do; to let your feelings loose. "Let joy be unconfined!" That's how I always feel, anywhere . . . which I guess means that I'm not really gay. Being gay, I gather, means that you can only show affection for people of your own sex, and only when you're among "your own kind"—and I've never felt that way. Maybe my parents were right, and this gay thing was just a phase I went through.

These wild-eyed straight-bashers continually raise the shibboleth of "hate crimes" that are being perpetrated against gay people, nationwide, daily. I'm very sorry for the speechmakers, but they need to adjust their Prozac dosage. I've lived most of my life outside San Francisco, sometimes in small cities, sometimes in rural areas, sometimes in between, and I can honestly say that I've never lived *anywhere* that made me feel unwelcome or in danger from the simple fact of being gay, or showing simple acts of affection in public. And we're even including about a year lived in Texas and Alabama—where, yes, I was once assaulted during an imprudent late-night stroll. *By two gay men.* Maybe they beat me up because they thought I was straight; who knows? No, I think this sort of twisted nonthinking is so far restricted to California. Can we establish a quarantine, please?

I'm having a hard time, here, swimming back to the shores of reality. Just who do these folks think they're helping, when they declare that a kiss is no longer just a kiss, but an act of terrorism and brutality? "You are an oppressor, whether you know it or not," the flyer stated. I guess this implies that I must be oppressed, whether I know it or not. Funny, I don't feel oppressed. Anyone who allows something as silly as this to "oppress" them doesn't have much of a self-image to start with, and hearing that they've claimed the Castro as their territory (I decline, vehemently, to share title with them) really does make me feel that I would rather not be called "gay" anymore, lest someone confuse me with loops like this one.

I'm not a politician or a singer or an actor; I don't have a nationwide TV audience for my statements of principles. I am a writer, and I use words, as effectively as I can. As long as this madness continues, I respectfully decline to be identified by the word gay, though I doubt that my behavior or habits will change much: I'm sure I'll spend just as much time in the Castro. I'll probably kiss a lot of people there, in fact, and most of them will be men. But no, I'm not gay. That's just a phase I was going through. Let's hope these shortsighted bigots can manage to grow out of it eventually, too.

Breaking the Rules

There's a whole flock of people out there these days (and I do mean flock, as in sheep) who seem to know just exactly how I should live my life. This is kind of disturbing: People who don't even know me are giving me advice on my sex life, on etiquette, on what risks I should and shouldn't be taking . . . it's getting hard to pick up any gay newspaper without encountering one of these activist/journalists who thinks he's Dear Abby. Yeah, Michelangelo Signorile and Gabriel Rotello are at the top of anyone's list of do-gooders these days—in order to live long and prosper, thou shalt do exactly as we say, you are getting veeery sleepy, etc.— but the trend seems to have proliferated.

Used to be, when I was a kid, it was my parents who thought they knew the best way for me to live. Their version was blindly following the Way of God. Uh-huh. Put on this blindfold, and the Truth Shall Set You Free. I took my freedom straight, thank you very much, and told my parents where to go and how to get there. No regrets. I launched myself into the gay community, because it seemed like the place where individuality was most valued, a place where I could be true to my natural urges . . . and so it was, for a while. Oh, there have been criticisms galore, from the usual folks who think I emphasize sex too much, but I can mostly ignore those. Anyone who's got time enough to spend their days worrying about how I'm living my life obviously lacks one of their own. The charitable thing to do would be to find that person a boyfriend (or girlfriend) to occupy his or her time. But charity has never been high on my list of activities.

In the last month, however, I've been confronted with several instances of people who seem to be entirely too sure of themselves. What's worse is that that they're sure of themselves precisely because they're nonparticipants: They allow themselves the conceit of thinking that they're speaking as objective observers. In other words, because they don't have lives. Last month, in Chicago, I ran right into the middle of what passes for a controversy in that city: A proposal to designate a portion of Halsted Street as an Official Gay Area, and put up permanent rainbow arches over the street. Okay, I know, it sounds silly, but some people were serious about it, and some others were just as adamantly against it. And who should step into the fray but a straight (openly, avowedly straight) newspaper columnist named John McCarron. "Gays need to confront their image problem," the column was headlined, and in oh-so-tolerant tones, he addressed the gay community as if we were children having a temper tantrum. Give up your sensual, decadent lifestyle, he urged; buy minivans and move to the suburbs, get a mortgage, and then maybe straight America will accept you. And most of all, he urged, get rid of those garish displays of prurience called Gay Pride.

Okay: Being admonished by an indulgent heterosexual is nothing new to me. I just think of it as envy, and I have a bit of advice in return: Before giving someone your two cents worth on how life should be lived, you might stop to inquire about how satisfied they are with that life. It's generally a mistake (though a very common one) to give advice to someone who's happier than you are.

So I laugh at Mr. McCarron, and move on; I don't live in Chicago, I don't have to deal with the results, whatever they are, of his commentary. But then I come back home to San Francisco, and encounter something very similar—not in the daily paper, mind you, but in one of the (allegedly) gay papers. (I won't specify the commentator's sexuality, since whatever it is, she's put it on ice.) In a recent editorial, she took aim at those awful sex obsessed gay men, and the way we keep shoving our sexuality down her throat. (Believe me, her throat is the last place I want my sexuality to be.) "Speak softly, and don't expose your big stick," she advised. The object of her ire was a flyer for a party, on the night of the Folsom Street Fair, called the Sex Ball; it featured a photo of a well-known porn star, taken by Pierre et Gilles, a couple of photographers who do know how to display an especially delectable dick. Okay, this essay isn't about how scrumptious Mr. Shaw looked, spread out across that flyer; it's about the hysterics which it produced on the editorial page of *Frontiers.* "What does this say about us as a community?" she demanded (in the third person, so as to avoid identifying herself too closely with the community she was criticizing). "What we say can and will be used against us."

I'm a lot less interested in what is said by these sexually oriented flyers and decadent displays of prurience than I am in living my own life, the way that seems appropriate to me. I long ago decided that anytime you start to live your life subject to "what the neighbors will think," you might as well just slit your wrists, because you can never please Mr. and Mrs. Busybody. So: Frankly, my dear, I don't give a damn what the world thinks. You are free to follow my parents on their Road of Good Intentions, but I won't be joining you. And even though I may not participate in either the Gay Pride parades or the Sex Balls anymore—both of them involving larger crowds than I find pleasant, and both lasting far too long for this weary queer's feet—it gives me great pleasure to know that they are both happening, reminding the world that we're not living by their rules.

Living by the rules. That's what they're talking about. I don't live by those rules; I haven't since I was a teenager. When I came out, it was with a declaration that the entire rule book was full of shit, and I was ready to make up my own rules. I've tried to do that, ever since. That's what being queer is all about, and no wannabe mommy in editor's clothing is going to put me back in the parental straitjacket. Sexuality may not be the whole of my personality, but neither is it a bargaining chip, to be traded away for acceptance. I have nothing against the monogamy and sexual restraint urged upon us by the mouthpieces of middle-class morality; monogamy and restraints can both be wonderful things. It's just the presumption that raises my hackles. The presumption that "Mama knows best." Hell, it's enough to make me want to start up a magazine about public sex, just to irritate them.

Doubting Death

We are dying of faith. My parents live by faith: Their religion tells them that it is one of the chief pillars of life, and on those rare occasions, years ago, when I used to try debating with them the existence of a deity, my rational arguments were invariably met with one weapon: Faith. Logic and reason did not matter to them; in fact, they were tools of the devil. Their devoutness was proved by their very resistance to such traps; they were God's Children because of their faith. It was a response that filled me with horror and revulsion then, and it still does today. Oh, I gave up all contact with their twisted way of life many years ago, but I've been recognizing some of the same attitudes in recent months, coming from quarters a good deal closer to home.

We have been told, about a zillion times over the past twelve or so years, that AIDS is a disease with long, lingering complications, caused by HIV/HTLV3/whatever you want to call it, *which will inevitably kill you.* We've been told this by our doctors, the people who, we are raised from infancy to believe, are next to that deity in infallibility.

I don't know the cause of AIDS. I don't know the cause of life, either; I'm just living it. I do know that I've watched far too many of my friends gaze trustingly into their physicians' eyes upon being told that they were going to die, and Believe. They've believed just as ardently as my parents believe in their afterlife. And it's no surprise that they're mostly dead now. Perhaps they're enjoying an afterlife; who knows. Some people name specific opportunistic infections of which their friends died; some people claim they died of AZT toxicity. I say they died of faith.

I don't mean to place the blame for this entirely on the doctors. We've got an entire world out there—news media, politicians, and yes, religious leaders—who can't say the word AIDS without adding, in parentheses, "an invariably fatal disease with painful, lingering consequences, acquired through nasty, dirty sex." Who can stand up to this sort of onslaught of universal opinion? In our world, which lives by public opinion polls, this sort of unanimity has all the power of scientific fiat. The only amazing thing is that we didn't all give up the ghost en masse, upon diagnosis. It took ten years of epidemic before we began hearing occasional lone voices protesting. "But I'm alive!" they said. "I've been living with this disease for x number of years, and I'm alive!" These voices have gained some authority recently; some people have taken notice. PWAs have begun to move back into the realm of the living, through the deliberately unfaithful examples given by some of our most visible members. But the doctors continue to assume that we'll all be dead within a year or two at the most, and most of their patients Believe.

This shouldn't be taken as an absolute rejection of the medical community. I still resort to their rituals on occasion. But I take their advice with a healthy dose of skepticism because I think that is, literally, the healthiest thing. I listen to their lectures; I chew them over, and I spit out about nine-tenths of what I hear.

Occasionally, we read a news report, or hear an anecdotal report through a friend, of someone who's been "cured" of AIDS. Generally it's through a revolutionary new treatment that can't be patented—you know the story. Often as not, it's only available in Tijuana. A few people try the cure; it fades from sight. The latest such episode involves a doctor who's gotten a major book contract to write about his self-cure. I withhold judgment on these cures; most doctors, of course, scoff at them outright, saying that they're "impossible." At the very least, I applaud the fact that there are people out there willing to doubt their imminent doom. Do I sound like I'm arguing both sides of the fence here, that one should have faith in quacks and shamans, nothing but skepticism for doctors? All I know is that doctors are offering us death, and asking us to believe that we have no alternatives. These quacks and miracle-workers are at least offering hope. Will I go to Tijuana? Thanks, I've already been. Seven years ago. No, I wasn't cured; I didn't go there with any expectation of a cure. I went primarily because it was the firmest way of establishing my independence from the Church of the Medical Profession; it was a big "Fuck You" to their Faith. My body may eventually tell me that it's time to die, but I decided I wouldn't be getting the news from a sympathetic fellow in a lab coat who would tell me I had thirty-six hours to go, as he starts his stopwatch.

Our world is full of miracles. I revel in them every day. I doubt that they are the work of any particular deity, but that doesn't make them any less miraculous. To classify someone's recovery from AIDS symptoms as "a miracle" is pure bombast. The miracle is that we aren't all dead already. Of an overdose of faith.

Loving Life

This is written almost two years after the preceding piece; in the interim, death has taken a holiday, and the doctors have stopped being so insistent about our collective imminent demise. We are appropriately grateful. There have been a lot of other changes, too. Two years ago, my health was approaching its nadir, my finances were in free fall, and I'd put my heart in permanent cold storage. But even then, somehow, in the darkest days of the bankruptcy filing for PDA Press, during the agony of dealing with my ex, and during those months when I lay in bed without the energy to move, somehow I kept my sense of optimism intact. It's something innate, I guess; I've never been able to shake it. Life, you see, even at its darkest, is still wonderful for me . . . and I can't avoid the knowledge that whatever travails I'm going through, they *will pass.* I know they will. And meanwhile, there are hundreds of things to distract me. Such as:

- The taste of a bowl of chicken won ton soup at my local cheap Chinese lunch counter. I marvel at my ability to get so much pleasure out of something that costs under three dollars, but there you are, I'm a cheap date.
- The feel of a freshly-washed cotton shirt against my skin.
- Swimming underwater: the sensuousness of water opening up around me as I probe its darkest recesses.
- Reading Cyrano's glorious speeches for about the thousandth time.
- Walking down the street and noticing shaved heads and close-cropped haircuts all around me, each one expressing something personal and intimate about the wearer.
- The smell of fresh manure as I drive past a dairy farm. (Okay, you probably had to grow up on a farm to enjoy this.)
- Feeling Tico nibbling on my earlobe. (No, not my boyfriend, my parrot. My boyfriend doesn't nibble my earlobe. And if he did, my response might be slightly different.)

- Watching the mating dance of the Dicrossus: The male spreading his fins wide, vibrating, showing off his best colors; the female pretending disdain, trying to swim away, only to have him dance around in front of her, saying, "Fuck me! fuck me! please!" (No, not my neighbors, my fish. Humans are seldom so direct.)
- Sitting on the beach at Land's End, feeling the waves pounding against the rocks.
- Looking around me at the naked bodies—not all of them young and buff, but all comfortable in their skin—displayed for maximum effect.
- Walking back up the hill, running my hand over the tree trunks worn smooth by a hundred thousand men's hands before mine, and feeling connected to them all.
- The totally safe suspense of wandering the shadowy hallways of an unfamiliar bathhouse, never knowing what lies around the next corner.
- Studying the visible tattoos on that beautifully muscled young man in a tanktop sitting next to me in the cafe. I wish I could go over to him and ask if he'd mind showing them all off to me, but that's more chutzpah than I've ever had, or am ever likely to have.
- The taste of a cappucino and croissant: The first coffee I've allowed myself in three months.
- Listening to Garrison Keillor.
- Silence.
- The car that pulls over so that the passenger can ask me, "Hey, where did you buy that leather jacket? I want one just like it!"
- "Not a Day Goes By."
- The feeling of being out on the open road on a motorcycle, in total isolation from the world and in total communion with self and steed: Surprisingly similar, I suspect, to what a really devoted equestrian feels when mounted.
- Planting seeds.
- Watching them sprout, one by one or en masse.
- Walking.
- Walking halfway across Washington, DC, following a cute young stud in jeans and black leather jacket—not expecting anything, mind you, just following him because I had an hour

to spare and couldn't imagine a more enjoyable occupation than watching his gorgeous ass cheeks flexing as he walked.

- Lowering myself slowly, and with agonizing ecstasy into a scalding hot tub after a long day of walking.
- Really fresh roasted corn on the cob.
- Depression. (Yes, really. Even depression, with enough melodrama, can be glorious.)
- Smelling a rose: not because of its smell, mind you, they all smell pretty much the same, and I'd rather smell a man's sweaty armpit any day, but because of the decadence and dandyism implied by taking the time to stop and blatantly smell a rose, in public.
- Knowing that people are watching me smell a rose, and drawing conclusions.
- A hundred other small pleasures that I experience each day, none of which are the least bit extraordinary, but which remind me, continuously, of what an incredible life this is.
- And probably most important to my *joie de vivre:* friends. Oh, boyfriends and lovers and tricks are all well and good, and it's true that most of my pleasures are solitary ones. But I'm not sure how much any of these things would mean to me if I didn't have someone who I could call up, every now and then, and say, "You'll never guess what happened today . . . "

I get the impression, though, that many people forget about, or disregard, these signs of life. Not everyone; I certainly have some friends who enjoy every bit of the passing show, who greet it with the delight it deserves. It's an art, and I guess I was born with a talent for it. I wish I could share it effectively, but every time I try to put it into words, the joy dissipates, and the words lie flat on the printed page instead of dancing around a maypole, as they ought to do. (Watching the leaves turn yellow and orange and red; the one maple in the grove that turns shocking red while all the others are still green.) I suspect that's the essence of most forms of art: Whether on canvas, or in a symphony, most artists are trying to get other people to share their emotions. Not all of those emotions are joyful, of course. Grief, anger, and despair often come into play. I dabble in each of them, from time to time, but it's joy that makes me most feel most intensely, and it's joy that I find most difficult to express. It's the solitary emotion, for me. The others are much more easily shared.

In a Former Life

He looks at me with wild surprise, and says,
"But—that is you!" He means the image on the wall,
a painting made ten years ago, of modest size
and not-so-subtle humor. I could ask him,
and I'm tempted to, "What tipped you off?"
but then I know I'd shudder at the answer.
Instead, I answer quietly, as other images
come flooding through my brain: So many
men, so many fantasies, I've been. Not quite
all things to all of them; that was my goal,
once, but I reluctantly admit I am no Superman.
This portrait—not my favorite—gives me innocence,
but then suggests—to my eyes, anyway—it's all a front.
How many men? I answer, quietly, "Yes. That was I."

November 11, 1996

Rarely Pure

Comparing my life to the lives of my friends and acquaintances, I'm reduced to a state of dim incomprehension: How is it that I escaped so much of the hell that so many of them seemed to go through? I refuse to believe that my parents had anything to do with it. They were pretty ordinary people in most ways, not too different from most people's parents; I get along with my boyfriend's mom better than I ever got along with my own. I hold the usual ration of resentment against them—primarily for specific things, such as having me circumcised—but there was no chronic alcoholism, no corporal punishment, no sexual abuse (aside from the above-mentioned slice). They were as uptight, when it came to sex, as it was possible to be. And yet when I finally hit the scene at age eighteen, I was quite possibly the least inhibited person in the bathhouse, willing to try just about anything. Twice. Where is the connection? How did I come from that stock? No, I don't have the answers. It's enough to make one believe in some form of divine intervention, however. Somehow, I was saved from their dreary way of life. Thank you, Dionysius.

This didn't trouble me through all my years in the porn industry. All I knew was that I was doing what I liked to do. It wasn't until the last year, in fact, that I started to seriously wonder about predestination and genetics and all those other explanations for what we become. It still doesn't exactly worry me—I yam what I yam, as someone once said—but I've had a boyfriend for comparison, you see, someone who is eleven years younger than I, someone who grew up in a wholly different culture, someone who has a whole different set of experiences and expectations of life . . . and who is so uninhibited as to make me feel like Sister Mary Thomas from the St. Aloysius School for Slow Learners. (No, I was not raised Catholic. I acquired the parochial school mythology strictly by osmosis.) There are many things that Chris has not yet gotten around to learning, but when it comes to sex, he's several grades ahead of me. I've given up all attempts to catch up; there's no point. It's obviously something to do with his age, and something to do with the era in which he came of age. But being around him, besides making me feel positively prehistoric, also makes me feel that there's hope for the future. If we could just raise a whole generation with his attitude toward sex . . . well, I suspect that all the gripes enumerated below would be history. I hope that I live so long; and I hope that I can have a hand in raising those kids.

Learning Lust

"Be in the world but not of it." I frankly don't know or care which book of the Bible this quote is from, and I don't feel like looking it up. I know that it was the watchcry that guided my parents' lives (and probably still does). About a year before I was born, with six kids already in the nest, they moved from Orange County, California, to rural Josephine County, Oregon, and bought thirty-eight acres in a sleepy little valley three miles from the nearest grocery. That's where I grew up: Without a television, without a neighborhood cinema to resort to on rainy Saturdays, without a corner newsstand where I could leaf through comic books. They did their best to isolate us from that dragon known as Popular Culture. And, I have to admit, I am mostly grateful for that isolated childhood. I feel I am healthier for not having watched *Three's Company* or *The Brady Bunch*. If that's cultural elitism, so be it. I don't mind being called a snob. My parents did occasionally relent and take us to a movie, but it was clear that this was intended as a special treat—and the movies were always Disney spectaculars (from the period before the pinko Commie fag takeover at Disney). I also recall visiting the future in-laws, shortly before my oldest brother got married, and seeing *South Pacific* on their TV. I don't think my parents quite approved of one so young being exposed to such racy material, but they didn't say anything.

You get the picture? I led a sheltered life. All my pop culture influences reached me under clandestine, not to say furtive, circumstances. When did I start reading science fiction? Probably in fourth grade, shortly after I'd become obsessively interested in sex. Andre Norton was the first SF writer whose work I discovered. I particularly remember one book that took place on a planet ruled by religious fundamentalists, in which the protagonist touches a sinful rod and is exiled to the forest, where his skin turns green and he lives without clothes. This one was fodder for endless masturbatory fantasies. It wasn't anything in particular about the novel—there were no explicit, or even implicit, sex scenes—but the overall mood of the piece made me want to be exiled to the forest with him. Romantic. It awakened that hunger in me that I eventually came to know so well, the hunger that I came to identify as the need to get fucked. And since reading was my escape from my isolation, I associated it with everything wonderful in the wide world.

Reading was the one external stimulus that I guess my parents didn't feel they had the right to forbid. They had a large library of children's and young adult-type books (acquired through six other children, remember), and they were indulgent with my own acquisitions. Mostly, until I was in junior high, I ordered them through a school-sponsored book-of-the-month club (I remember one particularly edifying novel about a rebellious adolescent who bought a leather jacket and started running with "the wrong crowd," but of course he eventually learned the error of his ways—my introduction to the potential for wardrobe symbolism). Later, as I grew more independent, I discovered the used bookstores in town, and began cruising the county library.

It was in seventh grade when I started hanging out with a group of other weirdos: Guys who traded *Star Trek* novels, guys who had computers (primitive ones), guys who actually liked school and took all the most advanced classes. Some of the best moments of my childhood, as remembered now, came from sitting in Frode Jensen's English class, listening spellbound as Mark and Doug and Curt talked about various *Star Trek* episodes. They loaned the books to me, and I quickly moved through the entire canon. They began calling me Spock, largely because of my legendary impassivity and my highly mobile eyebrows. (Lifting one of them inquisitively was all it took to send certain classmates into hysterical gales of laughter.) Eventually, though, attractive as Spock was, I moved on to the hard stuff. Tarzan.

The covers of the *Tarzan* novels that Trent loaned me were the closest thing to pornographic art that I'd ever seen. I took them home and jerked off over them obsessively. Even though the character in distress was always a damsel, my imagination was fertile and versatile. Just imagining what they did behind closed doors was quite enough. Discovering, a few years later, that Philip José Farmer was having the same fantasies, and writing them all down for publication, was one of my first clues that There Is No Such Thing As "weird" sexuality.

There were two other areas of what might be called Popular Culture that I managed to sneak into: Bible Books (my parents, of course, encouraged this at every turn, not realizing that it was the heroic illustrations of Samson, Adam, and Jacob wrestling with the angel that interested me), and comic books. I didn't have direct access to comic books in my childhood (and by the time I had the mobility to go into town on my own, I'd lost interest in such childish pursuits), but on three occasions, friends from out of state came to stay for large parts of the summer. The kids brought with them their comics, and though I was ashamed of my interest (and my parents were transparent in their rigid disapproval), I devoured all of them, at moments when I was unobserved. In vain I searched the crotches of the Silver Surfer and Spiderman for some telltale bulge. Surely, if these were supermen, they should have super penises, too? Alas, no; all drawn as flat as women. I began to suspect that it was part of the bargain: if you give up your dick and balls, we'll give you superpowers. Thus ended whatever fascination I might have had with power. Little did I know the kind of power bestowed by a mere nine inches of turgid flesh!

Okay, these are my primary exposures to that forbidden world, growing up. Were these images pornographic? Only in my own mind, I suppose. But I've heard enough stories from friends to assure me that mine wasn't the only dirty prepubescent mind. Friends who lay on the carpet in front of the TV watching Batman and Robin, rubbing themselves to their first climax while watching Robin straining against the ropes that bound him. Friends who found their validation in the defining differences of various science fiction characters, outlaws all, every one a hero who proved his worth to society.

All of David Gerrold's and Theodore Sturgeon's novels *(The Man Who Folded Himself, Godbody)* included pretty specific validation for gay readers. Samuel Delany went further, making sexuality such a non-issue that it was understood, in his novels, that any character might have sex with any other character, regardless of age, race, sex, or cleanliness. Barry Malzberg wrote a short story about jerking off in Zero-gravity—okay, it may have been about something else, too, but if so, I didn't notice. Since Brian Aldiss is primarily a science fiction writer, his *The Hand-Reared Boy* was put in the SF section of the local bookstore, even though it was pure pornography, with not the tiniest reference to spaceships. What was it about these SF writers? Even Robert A. Heinlein, Mr. Straight of the science fiction world, wrote *Citizen of the Galaxy,* about a homeless boy who gets adopted by a trading family, then inducted into the space military (some great mental images of him in the showers and the barracks), and eventually turns out to be the kidnapped scion of a fabulously wealthy family. Okay, this is a universal theme, I'm sure, and without the slightest overt sexuality; I found it (and still find it) incredibly erotic, and took it as balm to my isolated soul. I'd always felt like a kid who'd been born into the wrong family; reading this novel made me ache to find "my" people. And of course I eventually did, but it took time, and reading was the way I passed that time. Reading and jerking off, and running out into the woods to pretend I was a green-skinned tree-dwelling outcast, instead of just an outcast.

Everyone feels "different" growing up. Everyone feels like an outcast. Everyone feels shunned and hated at their high school proms. I'm convinced of this. The only difference for me was that it was all true. Once I was out in the world, nothing much changed. Therefore, growing up with that certainty of difference/alienation was the best preparation I could've had for the real world. I feel like it was an ideal childhood, in some respects. Mind you, I wish I'd grown up with a freer attitude about sexuality and my body. I would like to be more open about touching, hugging, shitting—all actions that set off major red-alerts in my brain, due to an overly-repressive upbringing. But if I had been raised in my own best of all possible worlds, where depictions of all types of sexuality had been freely available to me, and the adults around me cast no aspersions on my preferences, and really only cared that I make the choices which would bring me the most pleasure . . . well, I can't help but wonder if I wouldn't have grown up like the boy in the bubble, with no immune system: Subject to total catatonic shock upon my first exposure to the Real World. It's this dichotomy of which gay activists seem blissfully unaware: by legislating equality, they are not actually changing the real world, they're merely removing us from it, making us less aware of it, "protecting" us from it. I've never considered this a healthy idea. Yes, I want to change the world. I would like my neighbors to be unconcerned about the gender of my bed-partners (and I usually feel free of such scrutiny, whether living in San Francisco or Cazenovia, Wisconsin), and I would like the world to be accepting of public displays of affection. Real-world attitudes, however, don't change quickly. I still see articles on a weekly basis, from newspapers all over the country, that talk about men "soliciting" other men for sex, in terms that make it clear that this is the most despicable, degraded and debased act available to man. This will change. But I doubt that having our marriages recognized will do much for those of us who don't consider ourselves "virtually normal."

I suspect, however, that I have strayed from my subject. What was missing from my formal education was a sense of the joy and pleasure of life; a sense of the breathtaking beauty of the human body; a sense of the possibilities of camp and theatre and drama. All these things I had to learn on my own. Fortunately, I was taught independence in spades, so I was constantly aware of the limitations of my teachers. And yes, despite my reliance on the written word for my fantasies all through my formative years, it ended up being a movie that stands out as the dividing line between adolescence and adulthood. After sitting through three consecutive Saturday showings of *Star Wars* in our small-town cinema, I rode my bicycle home after dark in a dream-state, delirious visions dancing in my head of running my fingers through Luke Skywalker's long blond windblown hair. Luke left his backwater home for the big city, and look what happened to *him* . . . and from the perspective of 1997, it's easy for me to say that it was that moment that informed me of the choices available to a post-Stonewall queerboy. Okay, so Luke didn't marry Han Solo (or Chewbacca, which even at that age I thought would be more interesting), but he looked like he was having a lot of fun. Fun of which I was sure my parents wouldn't approve. That was good enough for me. I was ready to be of the world, thank you.

Do It Yourself

This is the way we beat our meat
Beat our meat, beat our meat
This is the way we beat our meat
So early every morning.

All right, class: Lesson number one. Attitude. In order for jerking off to be a truly satisfying sexual experience, you need to *expect* it to be. That's not so difficult, is it? But there is still a lingering prejudice against it, a snobbery, a belief that it's "not as good" as fucking. Get over it, boys. Speaking as someone who's had plenty of both, I can definitively state that the best orgasms of my life were by my own hand. You'll notice I said *orgasms.* That's not the same as saying "the best sex." Sex is an interaction between two (or more) people; jerking off is the pursuit of the Big O. You can make the hunt as leisurely or as hurried as you like (I've had j/o sessions ranging from two minutes to six hours), but when you're beating off, you're probably doing it with that goal in mind. And, notwithstanding all those stories in stroke books about "my first blowjob," and how "I didn't know anything could feel so good"—personally, I've yet to find a mouth or an ass that could tickle my dick the way my own hand can. This is not a put-down; in most cases, I'd rather be having sex with a partner. Climax is not the only pleasure. But the orgasm feels better if I'm by myself, so that I can concentrate on nothing but the pure sensation of my own climax, the sight of the cum shooting out of my piss-hole—instead of paying attention to my partner and whether he's getting off on it. It's a tricky balance.

So, my point? Loosen up. It's funny how so many sexually liberated leatherdudes, who think nothing of pissing on someone or licking their boots, find it somehow embarrassing to "admit" that they jerk off. Me, I don't have to admit it: it's well documented on film and video, and those with long memories may recall the glory days of Savages when I could cum twice nightly, onstage. Those shows . . . well, I wish I'd had the foresight to have a couple of them videotaped. I can't do that anymore. But it does give me a platform from which to examine the subject in depth.

My shows were generally forty minutes long—longer than most of the other performers. It took me a little longer to warm up, perhaps, but once I got going, I hated to end it. Giving them a good show was top priority. So I'd get up there, fully dressed: I had four basic outfits: Cowboy, military fatigues, "full leather," and what I called "sleazy leather." Boots were essential. For the first five minutes, I'd just "get in the mood": Strut around the stage rubbing my body through my clothes, showing off. Showing off is a big part of masturbation, whether it's to the guy in the apartment across the street, or to your own reflection in the mirror. I was lucky to have an appreciative audience, not available to everyone, but I encourage all of you to at least pretend that you're performing: Show it all off.

Then—I'd strip. I never tried to make it into a strip act; I never had breakaway clothing, or three layers of underwear. I just tried to maintain contact with the audience while I was doing it, taking off my clothes as if he and I were stripping for sex. The audience, you see, was really just one man, a man with fifty dicks, all being beaten off at the same time. Pretty sexy notion. So yeah, I'd stop at my jockstrap—I almost always wore a jockstrap, whatever the costume, just because it turned me on so much. That gave me a chance to strut around a little more, show off some more, show them my butthole. Play with it a bit. Get down on my stomach on the stage and stick it up in the air. That was always real popular: Seeing a "butch" dude getting down and begging for it like a bitch in heat. And remember, I'm still talking about masturbation.

Playing with my butthole has always been one of the most arousing things I can do to myself, especially if there are hungry men out there in the darkness salivating over the sight. But I'm doing it with myself, to turn myself on, and that's masturbation. Just because we mostly use the dick-oriented terms (beating off, whacking off, jerking off), a lot of guys kind of forget about ass-play, tit-play, toe-play. Don't.

Okay, so we're twenty minutes into the show by now, and they still haven't seen my dick. I've been rubbing it through the jockstrap, and if it's a good night, I'm more-or-less hard, but it's time for the "real" show to start. The reason most of them came here. The jockstrap gets hung around my neck, usually, so I can grab it with my teeth occasionally, and chew on it. Usually, it would take me another five minutes or so to work up to a real solid boner: The one that curves upward. Once I'd achieved it, though, it was easy to keep. All I had to do was look at my shadow on the movie screen behind me, the silhouette of my dick sticking out in front of me, larger than life, then poke a finger or two into my asshole—and I'd go into a frenzy. After a while, I hardly even needed to touch my dick. Just a stroke or two, then my hands could wander around my body, fingers exploring my ass or pinching my tits or spreading my buttcheeks for eager voyeurs, or rubbing my armpits and then sucking the sweat off—and this, all of this, is masturbation. The fantasies I had of that fifty-cocked man coming up on stage and raping me with every one of his cocks: Don't confuse that with sex. It was fantasy; it all took place in my head. In reality, not one man ever came up out of the audience and raped me. (Cowards.)

I've spent a lot of my life engaged in fantasies of various sorts, many of them violent. They've contributed to some of the best orgasms I've ever had. I won't deny that it's a little bit disturbing to me, when I'm no longer turned on, to remember some of the more intense fantasies I've had on my way to orgasm. But fantasies, all kinds of fantasies, are the very stuff of masturbation. Maybe there are some men who really, truly, don't fantasize, who concentrate only on the physical sensations in their dicks, but I wouldn't like to be one of them. Physical sensations are not where it's at, for me: In masturbation, as in sex, it's the thought processes that make it intense or boring.

So, I'd be standing there, in silhouette, probably up on the block that sat in the center of the stage, dick making a perfect upward arc . . . and that's when I did the "specialty" that made most of the audience gasp. Putting my hands on my butt, I'd lean over and capture the head of my dick between my lips. I could feel the audience sitting up to get a better view. Now, this is a subject of some contention: Is sucking your own dick masturbation? It doesn't involve another person, true, but it is "penetrative" sex. Well, hell, so's using a dildo. Perhaps the precise definition isn't so important.

It turned on the audience in a big way. Mind you, I was never able to keep it in there for very long: Five or ten seconds, and the strain on my neck began to outweigh the pleasure in my dick, and my hard-on would start to fade. So I'd go sit down and beat it for a while, playing with one of my boots, sticking the toe of it into my ass and rubbing my dick over the leather. Then I'd bend over again and suck it some more (it was a little easier in a sitting position, but not quite as impressive), and strut around the stage a bit, sniffing and licking my armpits (a major turn-on for me), and then I'd be ready for the finale.

First, I'd get dressed. (Huh?) Oh, not all the way, but I'd put back on some of the clothes I'd discarded. My cowboy hat, or my chaps and jacket, or mirrored sunglasses. Definitely my boots. Throwing my legs up in the air while I pulled the boots on, hard-on sticking up between them . . . I think of that as one of the best "shots" of the show, although I never got to see it from the audience's perspective. And then, half-dressed, I'd go into my final jerk-off, slowing down more and more, just barely touching my dick, strutting along the edge of the stage, sneering in friendly fashion at those men who I had in the palm of my hand, until . . . eruption. I don't need to describe that; you know what a cumshot looks like. And I modestly think that my on-stage cumshots were among my best ever. It got to be an art: Making sure I was in profile, so the audience could see the arc of cum; making sure some of it landed on my leather jacket; and of course the verbals. I've never been a noisy kind of guy, you know? I grew up jerking off in a house filled with sexually re-pressed people, and I always had to be absolutely silent. No moan-ing, groaning, or yelling. It hadn't occurred to me to change that, until I found myself onstage. Suddenly, noise became almost essen-tial—not just for me, but for the audience, to communicate to him my rising tide of excitement. Oh, I didn't actually talk to him, or spin dirty stories, or anything, but when I was in that preorgasmic frenzy, and I'd shove two fingers into my asshole, some incoherent yell would usually come out, and hearing it would turn me on all the more. (Yeah, *rape* me, you sonofabitch!) Making noise, I discov-ered, was one of the essential pleasures of beating off; it reinforced the news that my brain was already getting, *This Feels Good!*

And then, of course, after the final spurts and dribbles, it was time for the come-down. I'd keep playing with my asshole while milking my dick, sending more tremors through my body, and getting more grunts and moans out of me. Then at some point, my legs would start to shake (hey, it takes a lot out of you, doing that much physical exercise while walking around stage and holding poses and pretending to be butch) and I'd have to wrap it up. But never without a final acknowledgement of him, the audience. That's when I'd stare out at him and smile, as I licked the cum off my hand. Then pick up my jacket and lick it off, too, making it real clear just how much I loved eating my own cum. No acting required. Then I'd gather up the rest of my clothes, take a bow—grinning, exhausted, but happy—and off.

And they call this "work"?

Hey, I won't deny that I felt like I'd worked an eight-hour day digging ditches when I got home after my two shows, but at the same time, I was having the best sex of my life. With fifty men nightly. (Okay, sometimes a lot less than that.) Masturbation became, during that period, my major sexual outlet. Sure, I continued to fuck, and went through several affairs, and made a lot of movies, but it's those afternoons at home that I remember most vividly, afternoons with nothing to do, when I didn't have a show that evening. I'd put on a porno tape, spread out a beach towel over a bean bag chair, get out some of my favorite magazines and stroke books, dig into the Vaseline, and . . . go to it. I always used Vaseline because it lasts the longest. Three hours later, it's still there, still slick. Just applying it to my dick gave me a thrill: Something about the stickiness gave me an erotic charge.

These at-home sessions didn't differ so very much from the on-stage version, except that I didn't have to do it standing up. I'd go through most of the same motions—licking my own dick and armpits, playing with my butthole, etc.—but it was more comfortable, so I could go on longer. I never wanted it to end. And I discovered, with much experimentation, that two to three hours was the ideal length for a j/o session. The tension continued to build, in my body, up to about three hours; after that, something else happened, and I went into a slightly altered state. Not unenjoyable, and I occasionally kept it up for several hours more, but the orgasm, when it finally arrived, would inevitably be . . . anti-climactic. The sensations were still intense, but the cum would just pour out, instead of spurting, and it would be very thin and watery. After that many hours of pleasure, I guess my nerve centers were just over-loaded.

But! If I chose my moment carefully—and cumming has almost never been an uncontrolled, irresistible moment for me—some-where shortly after the second hour, I was capable of the most intense fireworks displays. Something up my butt was essential at these times. Usually just fingers, but yes, occasionally vibrators or cucumbers. I tended to prefer cumming while on my back, but sometimes I'd do it while kneeling, with my heels digging into my butt, just to see how far I'd shoot. Massaging my perineum as I shot, feeling that muscle spasming, always got an extra spurt or two out of me.

Jerking off, I'm happy to say, is no longer the solitary vice that it once was. There are social clubs all over the world that encourage it and promote it. I've spent many happy hours beating off with friends. But pleasurable as those times have been, my most intense erotic memories come mostly from those solitary afternoons at home with my porno and my fantasies. As my father (and probably yours, too) was very fond of saying: If you want something done right, do it yourself.

Candid Camera

One of the questions that I'm asked with some regularity, by folks who get beyond the "what was it really like to work with [x]?" stage, is the one about "the glare of publicity." "Did you ever have problems with stalkers?" or, "Don't you find it annoying, being recognized all the time?" The simple answer is No; I was just never that famous in the world at large, however central I may have been to the questioner's sex life. But I'd also always dismissed these questions lightly: I mean, there are certain trade-offs you make for having a famous face (or other body parts), and it seemed churlish to complain about the very thing that got me so many perks. Recognition may not always be good, but then, what is? I don't think it had ever really hit home with me until today just how serious that price could be. No, no one has ever hounded me into crashing my car; no one follows me around trying to sneak photos of my private life. For this, I am grateful.

In part, this is because there's nothing there to be revealed. Paradoxically, by living my life as openly as I'm able—by having photos of me in all my naked splendor available on the World Wide Web and at any corner XXX bookstore, not to mention videos of me doing all the things that most people spend their whole lives trying to hide—I've rendered tabloid journalism irrelevant. There's nothing they can reveal about me that I haven't already revealed. I fuck? Yeah, big deal. I get cucumbers stuffed up my butt? Yawn. My hair has been through more different shades and styles than a Vermont maple? Yep, it's all documented. Damn good thing, too, because I'm tired of most of it, and if there's one thought that bothers me, it's the nagging suspicion that I might have left something undone in life. Fortunately, there aren't a lot of such suspicions.

But that mere fact that I'm over it comes as close as anything, these days, to being my Deep Dark Secret. It's the thing that I have the hardest time explaining to people, without sounding like I've been born again. Really, this isn't a religious conversion I'm talking about; I view my salacious past with nothing but affection, and I'm thrilled to have it all out there on display. All I'm saying is: It's over. It was a phase, a very good phase, but nothing lasts forever. Now I'm exploring something else, something suspiciously close to—okay, I might as well say it; if I don't, those snooping tabloid photographers will find out about it eventually anyway—my parents' ideal of monogamy. Yes, I admit it: I have a boyfriend, have had for the past eight months now. In that eight months I've gone out and sucked someone else's dick exactly once, just to prove to myself that it was still possible, and mostly I proved just the opposite. (Possible, yes, but boring as shit.) I've even taken to wearing a ring on my left hand. No, we didn't exchange them in a commitment ceremony or anything, but it's intended as an indication to interested suitors that I'm "Unavailable." First time in my life I've ever wanted to send that particular message; first time I've even been willing to admit to it. Being unavailable, even for the evening, always caused me angst before; I didn't want to turn anyone down, lest he be the real Mr. Right. Having a boyfriend at my side, even if I was really and truly in love with him, always raised doubts. At the moment, there are no such questions in my mind, and it's downright frightening. I'm not used to feeling this degree of certainty in life. Will this change? I wouldn't be surprised. Everything else in my life has always changed. Nothing lasts forever, not even those lovely videotapes of me doing the nasty; not even a royal fairy-tale marriage.

Thinking about it, I realize how lucky I am to have gotten all these secrets out in the open. I could have lived the life of your average everyday Reverend Davidson, repressing it all, keeping it from sight. I can't imagine such a life of lies, but lots of people do still do it, and can't imagine anything different. Most of those lies are due to religious expectations that can never be fulfilled. Back to the basic premise: Do you really think those tabloids would have a market for all their innuendoes and stolen photos if the celebrities in question felt able to talk freely and openly about all those aspects of their lives? Okay, it isn't necessary, I suppose, for the royal couple to market videotapes of their wedding night (though, considering the state of the royal finances, it might not be such a bad idea), but this notion of eternal fidelity reads like a great big engraved invitation to the media—"Kick Me, Please!" And how did I escape such a fate? Very simple: I decided to be honest.

That's one of the primary reasons I'm making a habit of my boyfriend's twelve-step meetings. The people I meet there are honest: More honest than any group of people I've ever met. They're tired of hiding these things, pretending they don't exist, sweeping them under the carpet. They spend these meetings talking about those feelings, the urge to use, the urge to "act out," and the various depths to which drugs have taken them all. Not the sort of thing that most people like to admit to. Okay, I don't have stories that can compete with most of these guys. I hope I never do. But mostly, whatever the rest of my life brings—even if I end up staying monogamous for the next sixty years—I hope I'll never be so ashamed of anything I've done, so afraid of the glare of publicity, that I need to run away from the cameras. Cameras, with the advent of digital technology, may not be the absolute truth tellers that they once were, but they still offer a pretty good reflection of reality. Maybe it's possible for the truth to be overexposed, but I have yet to see it.

Through a Maze, Darkly

The seventies are generally regarded as an era of licentiousness and sexual excess: Bathhouses, discos, Fire Island, poppers, fisting, leather, cruising (and *Cruising*), backrooms, orgies. I regret to say that I'm not qualified to comment on most of this. I didn't set foot inside a bathhouse until May 1980; I never liked disco; I've still never visited Fire Island, and cruising, for me, was largely a matter of being totally oblivious. When you're eighteen years old, you can afford the arrogance of letting the other guy make the approach.

Still, latecomer though I was, I had time to dive into the hot tub once I discovered it. In the first three years of my debauch, I visited no fewer than forty bathhouses, scattered around two countries. I hope none of you will be so unkind as to make a connection between those peregrinations and the fact that many of them closed shortly thereafter. Believe me, I did my best to prevent their closure, both by patronizing them regularly and by political activism. None of it worked. Those that weren't closed by city edict eventually lost so much business, due to the hysteria sweeping the country, that economics forced their closure. It's one of my great regrets that I never got to see the New St. Mark's, in New York. By all accounts, it was the grandest of them all. I probably would have hated it. After all, the Steamworks in Honolulu—a tiny, rather dingy little place, about a tenth the size of the CBC San Francisco—will always remain one of my bathhouse ideals.

And just to put to rest one of those suspicions that everyone reading this chapter is bound to have: could I have caught AIDS at the baths? Well, of *course* I could have. In fact, I haven't the foggiest notion where I caught it, and it doesn't much matter. In a whimsical mood, I'll state that I hope I did get it at the baths: Because there are so many encounters from bathhouses that I remember with lust, awe, and affection. Let's say, just for convenience' sake, that I got injected with the virus on a certain night in late 1980, at Manscountry in Chicago (an improbably early date, admittedly, but a memorable one), when I arrived, showered, sat in the hot tub relaxing for a while, then went upstairs to the orgy room (pitch-black), felt my way through the masses of men to the far wall, bent over the carpeted and padded bench between two other similarly receptive men, and waited for the line to form behind me. I didn't wait long. I'd recently read a story, in some porn magazine, of a man who got fucked by thirty-nine men in one night; it had fired my imagination, and I was determined to equal it. (This scenario still gets me as excited as any other.) I have no idea how close I came; I kind of doubt that I got beyond ten. My asshole, while eager, has never had a lot of endurance. But ten is quite enough. Was one of them Gaetan Dugas? I kind of hope so. I like the rather improbable notion of having gotten it directly from "the source." Eventually, I know, asshole dripping with cum (another image that arouses me beyond all rational definition), I stumbled to my feet and made my way to the end of one of the other lines, to deposit my own load in one of the other greedy sex pigs.

Naturally, this is exactly the scenario that prompted Randy Shilts et al. to sound the alarm bells and force the closure of the baths. Were they the "cesspools of disease" that they've been called, in so many editorials? Well, only if you consider queer sexuality itself to be a cesspool. Many of these editorialists apparently do. Myself, I never felt so satisfied as when I stumbled home from the baths in the early morning light, grinning blissfully, Crisco squishing between my cheeks, tits so sore that my shirt was almost intolerable. I can well understand why such establishments must be eradicated: society does not allow that sort of unalloyed happiness. Heaven, as any theologian will tell you, can only be achieved through suffering. It has also been suggested, by those less charitable than I, that Randy only began his campaign to close the baths after the Eighth & Howard club (one of the ones with a restrictive door policy) began refusing him admittance. But in any case, I'm sure Randy would never have bent over a bench, waiting for a line to form. I'm sure he got his virus from a loving, caring, mutually supportive, intimate and monogamous relationship. In his bedroom.

But here I go, being bitchy, which was not my intent. Speak no ill of the dead, you know. It's also perfectly possible that I could have gotten infected from that man-of-my-dreams, with whom I was infatuated for all of six months. Yes, we were In Love. But somehow I doubt that a virus understands the sacred nature of such relationships.

The Baths . . . that phrase conjures up so many images to me. That orgy room at Manscountry, all tactile and aural, no visuals, is one of the primal ones. The hot tub downstairs is another. Baths, in my humble opinion, should always have a hot tub. Without it, you may call them many things, but they aren't bathhouses. And that medieval grotto at Manscountry . . . ! Dank and mildewed, condensation dripping from the ceiling, brick walls that looked like the original catacombs, with iron fixtures rusting away; who knows what bacterial menagerie lurked in the water? I loved it. Did I have sex in the hot tub? Undoubtedly—though the generally accepted practice was to catch someone's eye, then get out, spend an inordinate amount of time showering and drying off, then saunter over to the steamroom (with a meaningful glance back at your potential partner). Once inside the steamroom . . . well, my modus operandi was to lie face down on the bench that bisected the room. If my quarry didn't find me, someone else soon did. It hardly mattered. At the baths, a dick is a dick is a dick.

And that was one of the glories of the bathhouses, back in the—ahem!—Good Old Days: It really didn't matter. The only sin was Neediness, expressed as Pushiness. Yes, we talked disparagingly about trolls, but the term, I think, did not refer to an age or weight or appearance, but to an attitude, a lack of the proper sense of joy. Desperation has never been an attractive characteristic. As I've aged, I've come to accept it in my own life. On those nights (afternoons, mornings) when I feel most in *need* of company (and fucking), when I go to the baths or the bushes with a specific desire in mind—those are the times when I will find myself invisible. Shunned. Which doesn't help my mental state. The proper attitude for the baths is: Que sera, sera. If I get fucked, fabulous; if I don't, the sauna will still feel divine. I think I had that attitude down pat when I was lying on the bench in the steamroom at Manscountry; I've only had to remind myself of it a few times since. The essence of a bathhouse (besides a hot tub) is friendliness, camaraderie. In the really good baths, I feel the way an English gentleman of the nineteenth century must have felt upon entering his private club: This is my domain, they know me here, I can let down my guard and talk (fuck) with anyone, because anyone here will be of like mind. Not quite universally true, of course, but close enough. The towels spoke to that.

Ah, the towels! There is nothing quite like a towel. I guess the modern equivalent is the underwear party, but it's not quite the same. At an underwear party, one is still competing in a fashion show: If you're wearing last year's brand, I gather, you're scorned. But bathhouse towels are uniform, perfectly democratic; and thus, they disappear. They mean nothing—unless, as I always did, you wear them draped over your shoulder. Shameless, I tell you. I've always been a nudist at heart: As a young teen, I used to look forward to Sunday mornings, when the family was at church, so I could sunbathe nude on the back lawn. (See? Religion does so have a purpose!) And towels . . . well, they're an artificial construct, an effort to give people the comfort and psychological protection of clothing without its complications (shoelaces, buttons, zippers). But they've also taken on an additional meaning, an association with steamrooms and dark hallways, mirrors and mazes. Even in the darkest of orgy rooms, a white towel still stands out like a welcoming beacon; and if it doesn't outline the silhouette of a perfect butt, neither does it discourage wandering hands.

One of the more amusing features of many of the more elaborate baths (the Ballpark in Denver, the Club Ft. Lauderdale, most of the Midtowne Spas) was some form of maze. Now, I don't quite understand the reason for this attraction, but it's quite universal. We like to be lost. It's sexy. One of the best designed baths in the world is the St. Marc Spa in Toronto, because the hallways all branch and turn at odd angles. After spending a long night there, I still had to wander around for ten minutes before I could find the locker room. Call it "safe-danger." Everyone talks about how queers are danger-freaks, always looking for sex in the riskiest places. Well, the sensation of being lost (and then being "found" by your own personal Tarzan) provides a slight frisson of that feeling of panic—without having to strand yourself in the wilderness and subject yourself to the attention of *real* bears. I cannot recommend too strongly, to all of you out there who have an obsession with symmetry and long sight lines, that you stay out of this business. There are far too many heterosexual bathhouse owners already. What we need—what gay men, I am convinced, long for more than anything else—is a sense of uncertainty, of heightened suspense, and the exhilaration of a challenging new frontier. A dark orgy room; an unfamiliar maze; the opaqueness of a befogged steamroom, where faces only semi-materialize in the gloom.

The baths were an era; they were the symbol of adventure, and they were an education for me. Many men get their advanced education at college. University of Dallas did not offer courses in Advanced Queer Sex, so I dropped out and started going to the baths instead. The tuition was cheaper, and it was a lot more fun. It certainly prepared me for a different sort of career. And though there was never an official graduation ceremony, I think I can fairly claim the distinction of "Magna Cum Laude."

Soaking in It

My ultimate sexual fantasy—and them's strong words, coming from someone who is known for such things—is of bringing a guy home who fucks me, tenderly but firmly, who cums inside me, then pulls out and pisses on me. Without asking; without saying, "Let's go into the bathroom"; without any consideration for the bedclothes or the mattress. The essence of my craving for piss comes, I think, from the sense of breaking free from the bonds of civilized society, the Pleases and Wash Behind Your Ears and Use Deodorants. When I meet a man who doesn't feel that these artificial strictures apply to him—well, I probably won't ask him to move in with me, that would destroy the romance quicker than anything I can imagine, but I'd definitely try to see him again. And I wouldn't wash the sheets immediately, either.

Cleanliness has never been one of my ideals. A healthy body has smells; a physically active body has dirt on it. My gut produces gas, and when I fart I do not find the smell offensive. A dick naturally gets shit on it when it's in an asshole, especially mine (which is notoriously difficult to clean), and I see no reason why that should make me squeamish about sucking it, or about stains on the sheets. Natural body odors and products, right? Nevertheless, there are serious prohibitions against all of them. Piss is maybe a little less of a taboo than shit, but wetting the bed is still a major article of shame for many men. And I've bought into it for many years. Like most children, I was taught at an early age to keep a tight rein on my bladder. Throughout my teenage years, those sphincters were closed up tight. I was downright paranoid about letting go: Pissing at public urinals was virtually impossible, especially if there was a line waiting—like, say, at a football game, or a play, though play-goers were less likely to intimidate me than jocks. I would stand there, holding my dick, heart pounding, going red in the face, knowing that if I walked out of there without pissing, everyone would be staring at me knowingly, The Boy Who Can't Piss . . . and besides, the moment I walked out the door, I'd need to go even worse than before. These occasions were agony for me.

There have been a few times in my adult life—about ten, at best guess—when I've started up in the middle of the night, panic suddenly cutting off the flow from my dick. Each time, it was preceded by a prolonged dream of pissing: A dream that continued so long, it had the intensity of an orgasm. Once, this happened in another man's bed. That, I admit, was extremely embarrassing. We didn't speak about it in the morning, though he could hardly have missed the large wet spot on the mattress, but I never saw him again. I'd transgressed, gone beyond the boundaries of the social contract without permission.

When I got out in the gay world, it didn't take me long to find men who wanted to piss on me. It turned me on. I eagerly drank it. Then they always wanted me to reciprocate. I tried, really I did, but nothing came out. Again, there I stood, embarrassed. It was years before I learned to relax those inhibitions enough to let go.

Some of my favorite "practice sessions" have been associated with the open road. There was the time, eight years ago, when I was motorcycling around the country, and I was approaching Port Townsend, Washington, where I had the temporary use of an apartment. I knew I wouldn't have to stop for gas in the last two hours of the ride, and I was feeling, how shall I put it, "at one with the road," so when my bladder started sending signals, I decided that I wouldn't stop. Now, this is supposed to be a very Hell's Angels thing to do, pissing while riding—and I'm not that sort of rider. It took awhile for my conscious willpower to overwhelm my unconscious inhibitions. Every time I'd come close to pissing, my body would clamp down again— and the feeling of those sphincter muscles tightening was dangerously close to an orgasm. For twenty or thirty miles, it went on: I'd get close, get to that uncontrollable stage where you're sure you can't hold it back anymore, the piss would start down the tube . . . and then those muscles would clamp down, and I'd sort of space out for a few glorious moments. Okay, it wasn't a sterling example of good driving habits, but it was lots of fun. And when those muscles did eventually relax and let go, wow, I don't think I've ever known anything to feel so good. The pressure . . . ! Soaked my entire left pantleg and sock, got the bike all wet, and when I'd let loose with an especially strong burst, strong enough that I could see it bubbling out through the jeans and running down the outside, some of it would get caught up in the wind, and blow up into my face. Bliss. It could only have been improved if I'd had someone riding behind me who could've gotten as much fun out of it as I did.

The next year, driving cross-country again, I had a van. A 1964 Chevy Greenbrier, with vinyl seats. Like a lot of long-haul drivers, I spend a lot of freeway time jerking off, and this time, I decided I was going to cum when I was in the middle of the bridge across the Mississippi River. Hey, you gotta do something to make the miles pass. And, as usually happens shortly after I shoot a load, about five minutes later I knew I needed to empty my bladder.

Well . . . I'd already made the steering wheel sticky; why not see if I could wash it off? It wouldn't hurt the seats, or the rubber mats on the floor. So I held my dick straight up with one hand, and waited. This time it didn't take quite as long as it had on the bike: Having dick in hand gives the subconscious a little reassurance of familiarity, the knowledge that things are at least partly under control, that the piss isn't just going to go flying any old place. (And that's why pissing hands-off is such a charge for me, I suppose.) And I was becoming a little more relaxed by this time. It didn't take long. I washed off the steering wheel; then I aimed it up at my face. If I pinch off the piss-tube for a moment, I can get a truly spectacular fountain when I let go: I think I hit the ceiling of the van, and drenched my shirt and hair. And I was laughing like a crazy fool: it felt so damn good, so right and proper, to christen my van in that fashion. Pissing, even more than the cumload I'd shot just a few minutes earlier, established it as *mine*. Dogs have known this for eons.

After this experience, the floodgates were open. I'd suddenly realized the potential depths that could be plumbed in my psyche by just a stream of yellow. Living in the country, when I needed to piss at night, I'd just step outside and let fly wherever. On warm days, when I was working outside, I'd either just piss in my pants or take my dick out and spray it up onto myself. The sun would dry me soon enough. No, it really wasn't the same as having someone else do it to me, but the negotiations were easier. I dreamed of meeting another man with a similar lack of inhibition, a stud who would feel no hesitation about pissing on me across the table as we're having dinner; I yearned to live in a house that smelled like a urinal. I guess I'm a pervert, huh? Well, stop the presses.

I'm unlikely to ever find that particular ideal, the man without inhibitions, who doesn't observe the social conventions of politeness. (And if I did meet him, could I tolerate his other "uncivilized" habits?) But I would love to have a bed that's covered with stains, that conveys silently to any visiting trick the assurance that it's okay to let loose here, others have done it before you. I want to lie down on my stomach, and then feel his hot stream hitting my back, my ass, my hair; I want him to leave me soaking in it. Having done that, I suppose he could do most anything he wanted, next: Fuck me, beat me, spit on me, recite his poems, or just walk out. He would've realized my primary fantasy, and it would be difficult for him to top that.

It actually happened to one friend of mine—at least, so he says. It's envy that causes me to doubt him, slightly. Of course, it wasn't in his own bed: He'd gone home with a stranger, and was mightily surprised when the guy just let his piss fly. Not enough to actually soak the bed, but it didn't stay dry, either. Why can't this ever happen to me? There have been a few times when I've been lying in bed with someone, and he says, "I've gotta go piss," and I scoot down to his crotch and take his dick in my mouth, without saying a word, just looking up at his face with that begging, pleading look that all of you know so well—but each time, he asked, "Are you sure?" and I was forced to give consent. I don't want to be asked. I don't want a man who wants to know what I want. I want him to just do it.

Owning the Road

Jacket Number One

When my parents bought me my first motorcycle, I'd just turned eighteen. (Strange as it seems to many people, up to that point I'd bicycled everywhere I needed to go.) They were apprehensive, of course, especially since I'd also just gone out and gotten both my ears pierced, but they agreed that I needed some mobility. What we decided on was a six-year-old Kawasaki 350. And on my first ride into Dallas, I bought a jacket to go with it.

Why did I want a leather jacket? Well, for protection, obviously. One of the first lessons that's drummed into the head of any motorcyclist is: Wear protective clothing, because sooner or later you're gonna come in contact with the road. I've been riding pretty steadily for seventeen years, now, and due to good luck and caution, I've only hit the pavement three times; all three were at extremely low speed, and left me with virtually no marks. But I'm always aware that disaster could be around the next corner, so even when I lived in Hawaii, I never went out riding without my jacket. And when you depend on something that heavily—when you're continually aware that this second skin is what keeps *your* skin intact—it comes to have a degree of personality. When you suit up to go riding, you become a Motorcyclist: something similar to when Clark Kent becomes Superman. It's not a disguise, exactly, but it does change both the way you look at the world and the way that world perceives you.

I did not grow up with preconceptions of what leather "meant." I remember reading a story, in grade school, which used a black leather jacket as a symbol of a teenager's rebellion. I thought it was pretty funny, using wardrobe so transparently as a moral lesson. I didn't take it seriously. So that jacket didn't give me a sense of rebellion; it just gave me entree into the Dallas leather bars, and persuaded lots of guys that I was more experienced than I was.

That first jacket was pretty basic. Probably a Schott, I don't really remember. Cost around a hundred bucks. Nothing fancy, but for the next four years, it was my constant companion. I rode across the country in it, several times, and it stood up to a lot of foul weather. Then, in New Orleans, when I was at Mardi Gras with a friend, our van was broken into and the jacket stolen. Nothing else; we didn't have anything of value.

Of course I was in mourning. Leather isn't like other clothing. You develop a relationship with it; not only does it protect you, it molds you. In those four years, whether I wanted to or not, I'd become a leatherman (or leatherboy, as the case may be). I promptly bought another one.

Jacket Number Two

This one I bought in . . . was it Austin or Houston? I don't remember. I know we drove up to Austin after Mardi Gras, and in the leather shop in some bar (where I felt positively naked because I wasn't wearing any leather), I saw this jacket. It was lots more expensive than I could really afford—I think about $350—and it was called the Golden Bear. It had a "fur"-lined collar (I don't think it was real fur, but I'll never know) that could be snapped out; it had lace-up sides, that my old jacket didn't; it had a kidney belt. All the extras that I had recognized, over the previous four years of riding, were really worth paying for. I was smitten. I bought it.

This was during one of my bikeless periods; I was driving an old Ford van. Roaming the country, sleeping on a mattress in the back. When I arrived in Chicago, and was able to go back to the Gold Coast, site of my first debaucheries as a teenager, and show up there in real, grown-up leathers, I was proud as a papa with a newborn son. I kinda felt like I'd finally grown up. But the exhilaration didn't last long. I hit San Francisco a month later, and inside of a few weeks, the van had been broken into again, and my second jacket stolen.

Jacket Number Three

At this point, there was a certain amount of wariness to my actions. I don't think I phrased it quite like this, but I wondered if the universe was trying to tell me something. (Like, "Don't leave your jacket lying in plain sight on the front seat of your car in a big city.") I decided to hold off a while on getting a replacement.

For six months, I watched and waited. I studied the jackets I saw around me; in San Francisco, there was no shortage. Lots of them were real fancy. I tried on jackets in at least a dozen shops, both there and in Los Angeles. I never felt entirely comfortable with any of them. Until . . .

. . . yes, until I found that one perfect jacket, and our eyes met across a crowded showroom, and I fell irremediably in love. It was at A Taste of Leather: I think this was still the Folsom Street store. (It's moved twice since then.) When I lifted the jacket off the rack, I knew it was different. To begin with, the fucker was twice as heavy as any other jacket I'd ever lifted. I felt like I was at the gym, lifting weights. The leather was unusually thick, heavily creased: I was told that this was because it was horsehide. The salesman also told me that it was a Tauber, and he said this with a certain amount of reverence in his voice. The Tauber brothers, according to this guy, had recently retired, so we wouldn't be seeing any more of their jackets, but for years, they'd been the official jacket makers for the SFPD. Was any of this true? I've never cared to find out. I was taken with the jacket itself. Those lace-up sides, which allow me, with my rather narrow waist, to cinch it up tight to prevent cold drafts; the kidney belt, to support my back on long rides; the extra-heavy lining, which looked as if it would never wear out; the heavy-duty brass zippers; and the accordion pleats in the shoulders, so that the sleeves don't ride up your arms when you're reaching for the handlebars. This was a jacket designed for riding—and obviously a jacket designed for protection.

I bought it. I don't think I bought it that day; I think I came back about three times, trying to make sure it was the one I wanted. Again, this was an expensive one. I had an apartment by this time, so I didn't have to worry about the van being broken into. But I still didn't have a bike.

For the next three years, in fact, I was a biker without a bike. I was living in San Francisco; who needs a vehicle in the City? It's more trouble than it's worth. I take that back. For a brief period, I did have a bike. It was a Honda CB500T, in marginally rideable condition when I bought it. I only rode it once, on an aborted trip out of the City. I got hallway across the Bay Bridge, became very worried about some vibration or noise it was making, and turned around at Treasure Island and came home. I don't believe I ever got it running again. As I was saying: Who wants a vehicle in the City?

But I still faithfully wore my leather. All the time. Leather still felt natural to me, in a way that no other jacket could. I had hotter blood then, perhaps; nowadays, I need a down jacket on San Francisco's colder nights. But then, my jacket was the perfect badge of how I felt. I often wore it onstage when I did my jack-off shows at Savages: I had a regular routine, with the jacket and a pair of tight leather pants and a tank-top: after I'd stripped, I'd rub the tank-top all over my body, spread out the leather jacket on the platform, lie down on it to play with my asshole, then put the jacket back on to strut around the stage a bit—and when I came, I'd always make a point of shooting on either the leather pants or my jacket. Then I'd lick up the cum. A cumshot looks especially impressive against black leather.

During all the time I've lived in SF, I've never been assaulted. (Touch wood.) I've spent a lot of time walking through the Tenderloin late at night; I've walked through the Mission and the Western Addition, two neighborhoods commonly considered "dangerous," at all hours. I don't feel threatened by any of these areas. But then, I've also prowled New York's Central Park after midnight, looking for sex, and never saw the slightest sign of violence. And yes, I think my leather jacket, and the confidence it gives me, has a lot to do with this odd sort of immunity. I wear leather because I love it, because it is comfortable on me. But I think perhaps even if I didn't love it, I would wear it simply as a practical matter. When I'm in leather—the more of it, the better—I feel protected.

This is not the most realistic of feelings, of course. When fully encased in leather, movement is uncomfortably restricted. Ever tried running in motorcycle boots? Can't be done. But then, that's part of the psychological advantage: Leather slows you down, which makes you appear self-confident and challenging. Invincible. Strutting down the street in full leather always reminds me of a bumper sticker I saw many years ago: "Yes, as a matter of fact, I *do* own the road."

Sometime during this period, probably about a year or two after I'd bought Jacket Number Three (I remember it still being new), I visited my family. While I was showing off my jacket to them, I was stunned to see my older brother Donald—the staid, quiet, conservative one—come out of his bedroom wearing an almost-identical biker's jacket. We strutted at each other like peacocks in heat. I was jealous. I'd bought mine off the rack; his had history behind it. You see, my grandfather had recently died, and my brothers had done the housecleaning—and, among other things, they'd found this jacket. Who knows how old it was. Still in good shape, though. The lining was red nylon; the shoulder epaulets had little chrome stars on them. Now, I'd known that Grandpa had owned a bike, an early-1950s Indian; my father often waxed nostalgic about it. But my only personal point of reference to the old man was a photo of him sitting behind a desk, stern as Jehovah, with his hand on a Bible. It's hard to fit those two images together. I wish I had a photo of him decked out in leather, astride that mean machine.

I've had two more bikes in the past ten years. Between the two of them, I guess this jacket has ridden close to 50,000 miles. It's been soaked more times than I can remember, many times with rain, occasionally with piss; I'm happy to say it's never experienced any road rash. But in the past couple of years, it's begun to deteriorate drastically. I always took the best of care of my leathers, saddle-soaping and oiling them at least once a year. During my years in Wisconsin, though, when I didn't get out on the bike for long periods of time, I mostly wore my down jacket. The leathers hung, abandoned, in the closet. And the yoke, the area just behind the neck, began to break down. At this point, it looks like I've taken a slide down the road on my shoulders—an embarrassing impression to give, at least to other bikers. I'm gonna have to get it fixed, somehow. The cuffs are going, too; the lining of one sleeve has been half ripped out. But I'm not ready to give up on this jacket yet. Too many memories, too much confidence.

Memories? Well, of course I've had sex in it. Dozens, if not hundreds, of times. Those times when I'm out in the park, and I just go down on my knees—or down on my stomach—and I feel him gripping me through the armorlike protection of my jacket: I won't say that being stroked through leather is the most intimate I've ever been with another man, but it does give an external expression to a very masculine need to be impenetrable (while being penetrated). Even more often, I've taken it off and used it as a pad, to keep the stones from digging into my back. The times I've brought someone home, and we've had sex before getting to the bedroom, without ever taking off any of our clothes—I don't know if this has anything to do with leathersex per se, but it's one of my favorite fantasies. And those few times in the past ten years when I've ventured into gatherings of leathermen, whether at a bar or some other venue: In a crowd, the rubbing of leather shoulder against leather shoulder is very stimulating. Especially if he happens to be wearing chaps with bare buns below. The contrast—absolute armor with total exposure—is titillating for both wearer and viewer.

Many, if not most, leather jackets are heavily personalized. Patches, nametags, bar insignia, what have you. That's something that never really appealed to me. There are only two "custom" touches that I ever applied to my jacket: First, a pin that I wore for several years above my vest pocket that said "HEAD BOY"; and second, a cockring-type device that I wore (as a joke, appreciable only to my close friends) on my left epaulet. I say "cockring-type" because it was emphatically not a cockring: if I'd worn it as one, someone would've ended up with chipped teeth. It was an old copper gear, from the inside of a marine engine. I found it on the beach in Port Townsend, Washington, heavily pitted and corroded. The teeth on the outside were rather frightening, and it gave me an entirely false aura of roughness. I've always liked creating (and then destroying) false impressions.

What makes the perfect leather jacket? Well, to turn an old saying on its head: the man. You need to be comfortable with your leather. I suspect there are a lot of "leathermen" out there who wear leather just because they're trying to fit in with the leather crowd. They shouldn't feel the need. I know there are many *real* leathermen who'd like nothing better than to collar a nice respectable young preppy guy and drag him home. Comfort is the key. I am comfortable in leather (except of course on those forty-below San Francisco summer nights)—primarily because I "grew up" in it. Not only that, it gives me confidence. It gives me security. It gives me protection. It reminds me that I *do* own the road.

Performed Consent

In 1981, when I was barely twenty years old, I bought myself a video camera. Try to think back to 1981: It was a pretty primitive model, large and clunky, and required bright lights to get a decent picture. Still, what I immediately used it for (and pretty much the only thing I *ever* used it for) was a video of myself jacking off, in my tomblike basement studio apartment. It didn't come out very well (dark and muddy, sliding shadows: Very Artistic), but I didn't learn that for nearly a year, when I finally got around to buying a TV. By that time, I had quite a number of tapes of myself jacking off, shaving my head (and crotch), and performing various other titillating personal rituals. It wasn't until 1983, however, that I first set it up to catch anticipated sex with another person.

I still have all those tapes. Given my eventual career as a porn-star, I presume that they're marketable, however poor the quality. Hey, I expect there are those who would pay extra for "the *private tapes* of Scott O'Hara!"—and feel richly rewarded when it became obvious just how amateur this particular exhibitionist really was. To date, I haven't even tried. My marketing experience is nil, and I'd rather not enter this particular field.

In subsequent years, I did a lot of stage performances. Simply put, I jacked off. I never pretended that what I did was "dancing"; I never tried to make it into Art. I just tried to get men off, and I was pretty successful. Occasionally the subject would come up, among friends. Usually in joking fashion, someone would make a comment to the effect of "If you could write your performance up in a grant proposal, I bet you could get the NEA to fund it!" I was always the first to laugh at such suggestions, but in retrospect it seems likely that I could have.

From my own case history, let me digress momentarily to that of Scott Taylor, one of my colleagues who achieved perhaps not quite as much fame as I did (I don't know how many films he made, but only two—*How to Enlarge Your Penis* and *Strange Places, Strange Things*—made a significant dent on consumers' checking accounts), but at least as much local notoriety. In San Francisco in the mid-eighties, he was probably more recognizable than I was—and therefore, we were frequently confused. I learned not to say anything when someone complimented me on some performance that I was pretty sure was his.

And just what was his performance? Oh, it varied immensely. One of his shows involved being publicly "crucified" to a hurricane fence during a South-of-Market street fair; another included sticking a rather large and lethal-looking knife into his urethra. In spaces that were appropriate, his shows invariably included an orgasm. It would be wrong to say that they "climaxed" with orgasm; although it may have been in the Nob Hill's contract that he had to cum during every show, I don't think many of his fans went to see his shows with cumshots in mind.

What I considered the climax of Scott's Nob Hill show was the bit where he inserted a lucite rod, perhaps the thickness of his index finger and eighteen inches long, into his urethra. Now, catheterization per se doesn't hold many charms for me, but this was a hollow, sealed tube, filled with (presumably) red glitter and glycerin, and after he'd played with it awhile in an upright position, he'd flip his dick downward, and the spotlight would show us a vivid cascade of red coming out of his piss-slit—it never failed to get some response. And just in case that didn't chase 'em out, he'd follow this up with verbal threats to the audience: Flashing his knife, talking about coming down into the audience and cuttin' off some balls, that sort of thing.

Offstage, he couldn't have been a nicer person.

I decline to state whether I consider Scott's shows to be porn or performance art. I will say that I wish I had a videotape of some of them.

What we're dealing with, here, of course, is a matter of semantics. Definitions. Since porn has been my business for most of my adult life, I've had to put in a good deal of thought as to just what it is. This definition may not jibe with yours, but it's the considered position of a professional: Porn is anything—*anything* that is created with the intent of sexually arousing someone. Now, when I was twelve years old, I was cutting out the underwear models from the newspaper ads and gluing them into collages with each other—and though I was doing this expressly for myself, with no intention of arousing my mother (the only other person who saw them before she burned them), it was very clearly pornography. My pornography. (Since I was a child, I think this qualifies as "child pornography.") The *Bible,* while clearly obscene, I would never characterize as pornographic—except perhaps the Song of Solomon. (Hey, the "your legs are like towers of ivory, your breasts like leaping gazelles" school of porn has never done much for me—but I think we can agree that arousal was the writer's intent.) On the other hand, *The Bible,* starring a breathtakingly beautiful Michael Parks as Adam. . . . Tom of Finland was very clearly creating his work to arouse. Mapplethorpe, I tend to think, was creating his with shock value in mind (though he explicitly denied this). And Holly Hughes? Well, I never saw her earlier shows, but judging from *Clit Notes,* her most recent, I'm afraid I must deny her the title of pornographer. Oh, she's good; she's just not that *sort* of good. Her intent, I think, is to educate and entertain. Very different. I don't mean to be insulting, but I think she has redeeming social value.

Obviously, I'm not reading from the same dictionary that Jesse Helms uses. (Come to think of it, do you suppose there *is* a dictionary with few enough words in it that he could read it without being Shocked and Appalled by its obscenity?) But if you think defining "pornography" presents a problem, wait'll we get to "performance art."

Before we do that, let's step back another moment for a closer look at "intent." To return to my previous analogy: No, I don't think for a moment that the marketing department at Montgomery Ward was composed of pornographers. Oh, they were looking for arousal, all right, but they were targeting the right hip pocket, not the left front pocket. (And a stray thought occurs to me: Am I underestimating the market savvy of early seventies marketing departments? Were they perhaps aware that by stimulating the libidos of prepubescent boys, they were ensuring, if not brand fidelity, at least model fidelity for the next sixty years? Because despite the fact that I wear underwear in public about once a year, usually when I'm wearing nothing else, I still occasionally buy a pair of briefs, just to get a whiff of that new-briefs smell, and to put them on and feel that comforting snug-fit feel . . .) On the other hand, I do maintain that they were creating, whether or not they were aware of it, *erotica.* That is, *material that someone* (LOTS of someones!) *found erotic.* I find lots of things erotic that the creators may not have intended that way. That stuff, to me, is erotica. When I jack off on it and send it off to my pen pal, it becomes pornography; I have redefined it, Pornographied it if you will . . . which is one of the things Performance Art seems to be all about.

It may seem to a lot of you that I'm placing a lot of emphasis on intent, rather than content. *Isn't it the content that is pornographic?* I hear you ask. Nope, not by my definition. And if you use that criterion, I think you'd have to rank the Kinsey research, together with quite a lot of scholarly work since then, as pure porno. Hey, it gets *me* off when they start talking about frequency of ejaculation for fifteen-year-old boys . . . though admittedly, it would help if they'd just include a mention of what kind of underwear the boys were wearing.

But seriously, folks . . . back to the subject I've been avoiding, Performance Art. I've seen a few folks in my time who called themselves PAists; I liked some, hated some. I can't remember even one of them who I thought qualified as a Pornographer. There were several who sought to shock; more who intended to entertain. The latter category tended to be the ones I liked better. The one time I can recall when I've seen pure pornography presented on a stage as Art, it was actually called Theater. It was Robert Chesley's play *Jerker,* and I was vibrantly, intensely, sexually aroused from the first phone call to the end (and not only because the actors were wearing briefs). But we can't call it Performance Art, because there's a written script, which can be performed by just *anybody;* it's not performer-specific.

So there. I guess that's one of the criteria I use to define PA. I can't take Tim Miller's monologues and perform them; even if he were to allow it, I don't think it would work. The power of PA comes, in part, from its authenticity, from the audience's knowledge that This Is Not An Actor, This Is A Real Person (with apologies to the actors in the audience).

So if we combine those two definitions—Pornography is work intended to arouse, and Performance Art is authentic, performer-specific entertainment—I think we come to something of an impasse. Maybe I, after a dozen years being actively involved in various aspects of public sex, could create a show that satisfied both criteria; I don't think very many people in this world could be that public with their private sexuality. Oh, there are millions of comics out there (okay, it only *seems* like there are millions) who like to make jokes about their date last night. Sometimes the joke is even on themselves. But they're intending to amuse, not arouse. If you ever meet a comedian who can take his sex life seriously, and talk about it in a way that turns people on—well, to begin with, he's not a comedian, he's a pornographer. He's also probably unemployed. But I've never met anyone—with the possible exception of Scott Taylor, now alas deceased—who could effectively eliminate that public/private dichotomy around sex, and do so with Art.

Bottom line? Although theoretically there isn't any conflict between the two categories, in our current sex-phobic climate I can't think of anyone who even attempts to confuse the issue by straddling the line (wherever it is). It just wouldn't be profitable. And one of these fields of endeavor (I don't think I need mention which one) is most definitely profit-driven. Could that actually be the fundamental difference between the two?

Hot Nights in the Deep-Freeze:
Porn in the Nineties

Katharine Hepburn is alleged to have said, in reference to pornography, that sex couldn't be acted. Blasphemous it may be, but I agree with her. Oh, not literally: Yes, sex *can* be acted. Look at Jeff, or Rex, or Ryan. I just don't like the result. And unfortunately, that's the Philosophy of Porn that predominates, these days. Get a good-looking model, tell him to close his eyes and think of Sharon Stone. Gay men'll salivate, and cash register bells will start ringing.

There were videos, once upon a time, in which the actors didn't appear to be acting. I get out my videos from the seventies and early eighties, those Joe Gage films and the scenes between J.W. and Jon King, and some of the early Falcon product, and it seems to me as if the camera just happened upon a sex-scene that was inevitable anyway. I don't know how it worked, back then, but I know that all those actors were gay. Not bi, not straight, not I'd-rather-not-label-myself: Gay. And proud of it.

There's another change, over the past fifteen years, which may be related: The rise of AIDS, and the subsequent adoption of condoms. For several years, in the mid-eighties, porn producers were generally reviled for their "irresponsibility" in not using condoms; I was part of that era, and I was unsafe with the best of them. Then, sometime in 1988, everything changed. Perhaps the well-publicized deaths of a few pornstars made producers think about the publicity they'd get if the star of their latest epic were to croak before it was released. Whatever. Suddenly, directors were desperately looking for ways to make condom usage appear natural.

Ten years later, they're still trying. I have news for them: Condoms aren't natural, and they're not fun. And expecting porn actors to use condoms, ignore the camera, and pretend they're enjoying themselves . . . well, I don't know anyone who's capable of all three.

Many people will be protesting, in response, "But sex *isn't* the carefree, hedonistic pleasure that it was in the seventies! We have to be careful nowadays!" And they're right . . . from the perspective of those Negatives who want to stay that way. Fortunately, I'm Positive, and therefore not bound by those narrow strictures. I don't want to limit myself, and I don't want to see careful, safe sex on my TV screen, either. These straightboys who just have gay sex for the money are too depressing for words. They seem determined to let us know that they're not really enjoying themselves, and that of course they never do anything that might put them at risk of . . . well, of anything.

What worries me most about these emotionless exercises is that porn is, as we all know, educational. And I don't like the thought of our younger generation learning that sex is supposed to be like this. I blanch whenever I hear someone in a darkroom saying, "Yeah, suck that big dick." Let's start with the (non)possessive pronoun: It's not *that* big dick; it's *my* big dick, or *his* big dick, or *her* big dick. ("Big" being a strictly relative term, we won't deal with the necessity of using it.) I really don't want to see our wonderfully diverse sex culture turning into a bunch of Jeff clones, with personality displacement issues.

You know what I want to see? What I really long for is some nice, down and dirty, raunchy porn between a couple (or a group!) of Positive guys who no longer feel paranoid about those wonderful "bodily fluids." I know why such videos haven't been made, and it *isn't* because Positives don't do it. It's because producers (and educators, and social workers, and a whole list of socially responsible people) are afraid that if Negatives see these videos, everything they've been taught about safer sex will go right out the window and they'll start a massive orgy that won't end until they all drop dead of exhaustion. Yeah, well, that's what *I'd* do if I'd been denying myself for the past decade, and I suddenly got "permission." (The relationship between the gay community and health professionals, in recent years, reminds me of a game of "Mother May I.") What I want to see is a pornflick where all the participants *like* to suck dick. This doesn't seem like such a difficult task, really, but most current porn seems to be actively avoiding it, capitalizing on the supposed gay fascination with the unemotional, unresponsive

Butch Male. Rub two of those sticks together, and you don't get enough heat to melt a popsicle. Why should it be so difficult to find combustible combinations?

There have been exceptions—but they've been notable mostly because of their rarity. Artie Bressan, when he was alive, produced some of the most genuine porn I've ever seen. I've never been certain whether this was because he also did "mainstream" movies, or if he did mainstream movies out of frustration with the limitations of the porn genre. Cause-and-effect can be so confusing. Brad Braverman, in his four videos, walked a tightrope stretched between porn and art cinema: I think he succeeded on both counts, but not everyone agrees with me. His movies were, however, seized by the LAPD, which is usually a pretty good litmus test of fine art. (His photos were incredible, too: I was particularly enamored of a series of autoerotic suicides.) And then there are all the films of Jerry Douglas. Again, his level of success is open for debate, but I do know that his aspirations are a bit higher than the norm, and I admire him for that. To the extent that they fall short of their goals, I'm willing to lay the blame at the producer's feet, or perhaps the editor's.

Now, I've never been a director or producer. I'm sure they have problems. But I think the biggest problem they have is simple blindness. "That's the way it's done" seems to be their operating dictum. And I don't think it's good for the long-term health of the genre. AIDS may kill individuals, but it takes narrow-mindedness and conservatism to kill an industry. And I fear that porn is hovering on the brink. How much longer will we keep on supporting an industry that has all the imagination and daring of a White House spokesperson?

In Love with My Work

When I showed up at the hotel room door of my first official "trick," I was terrified. Not of him, *per se,* or of having sex for money, and certainly not of getting AIDS (this was 1985, I think; I probably already had AIDS, but just didn't know it yet), but quite simply that he might be a vice cop. I still don't know how realistic this fear was. All the hustlers I've talked to downplay the danger, at least in San Francisco, but I think most of them don't share my special antipathy to the police, either. Just seeing one makes me burn with anger, and I'm seriously afraid that being arrested by one of those scumbags might make me do something foolish, like try to kill the fucker. And I really don't want to spend the rest of my life in prison.

Just so I can get these opinions out of the way at the top of the chapter: The voluntary exchange of sex for money is a damn fine idea. Vice cops all deserve the electric chair. AIDS is nothing to be concerned about. And monogamy sucks. These are basic premises in my life, one or more of which may well irritate you. Too fucking bad.

As a sex-professional I was, frankly, quite an amateur. I never took a job that I didn't want to take; I never felt coerced into sex "for the money." I had all the money I needed to live modestly; when I started making films, I did so because I loved doing it. And when I put that ad in the *Advocate Classifieds* (the one and only such ad I ever placed), it was because I was eager to discover what the world of hustling was like. Terrified, yes, but very curious.

I didn't answer very many calls. That is, I got a lot of phone calls, but most of them were jack-off callers, late at night. Not very entertaining. I only made dates with three tricks—which was just about enough to pay for the ad. All of them were out-of-towners; all of them were perfectly nice men; but I discovered that sex isn't really very much fun when you're vibrating with tension, wondering whether he's gonna pick up his badge at any minute and flash it at you. Ruins the sex. At least, it did for me. I couldn't just relax and enjoy it. So I stopped running the ad. I kept getting occasional late-night phone calls, though, for the next six months.

It was the live performances and the films that I found much more satisfying. At the time, I'd never heard of a performer being arrested for prostitution (I think it's been tried once since then in Los Angeles, but I don't know the outcome of the case), so I felt pretty safe. And as I told people, repeatedly: when I trick with a client, I'm satisfying one man. (Well, two—presumably.) When I'm up on stage, I can watch dozens of men jerking off over me, I can see the lust in their eyes, the need in their gonads. But when I make a video, I'm satisfying thousands of men, possibly millions in the decades to come. That's worth something to me. I'm happy to be able to report that, ten years later, it's still true: men are still watching many of my videos, they're still jerking off to them, they're still telling me about their favorite parts (and critiquing some of their less-favored parts), and I still get an incredible charge out of knowing those facts. Not many men get the chance to give pleasure to as many people as I have; that's a better payment than any paycheck.

Oh yeah—money. You wanted to hear about the money. For films? Well, the first film I did, I think I got paid $150. The top dollar I ever got paid was, I think, $2,000, and I had to do two scenes in that film (or was it three?). We typically got paid by check, but the director was happy to cash our checks on the spot if we insisted. For jack-off shows, I think I started at $35 per show, and worked my up, eventually, to $1,000 a week. Which was not actually that much of an increase, since during those one-week engagements at the Follies and the Show Palace, I was doing two, sometimes three shows a day. Fortunately, they didn't require an orgasm at each show.

For the rest of those years, I was a pretty regular performer at the Campus Theatre in San Francisco. There, I think I was eventually paid something like $75 per show. Hey, not bad for a thirty-five-minute show; that's almost lawyer's pay. (And lawyers, remember, work at those wages making lots of people miserable!)

Sometimes, an audience member would hang around afterward and offer me money to have sex. I'd usually brush him off—but more than once, when I found him attractive, I said, "No, I won't have sex with you for money, but I'll do it for free." A couple of them took me up on it; a couple others turned me down, to my surprise. And it took me awhile, but I finally realized that my response was turning them off. These guys wanted validation for their economic choices, as much as for their appearance. When I told them that I didn't want their money, the subliminal message was that sex with me wasn't *worth* paying for; that they were stupid for offering. So the next time I got such an offer (it happened to be from a regular customer, who I'd seen in the front row jacking off on a number of occasions), I just said yes. He told me that all he wanted was, literally, a private show. Usually that's a euphemism for sex, but he just wanted me to jack off for him, in his living room, in front of his mirrored wall. And I did, gladly. It was a fine show— I took along my boombox and performance tape, and did my show exactly as I usually did it onstage—but I have to admit that the drive back into the city afterward was a bit uncomfortable. Still, I got the impression that he got exactly what he wanted, and like I say, that's a satisfying sensation. What did he pay me? I haven't the foggiest idea. I probably asked him for the same fee I was getting from the Campus at that point. Getting paid for it didn't mean much to me, frankly, but paying for it obviously meant a lot to him. It meant that I was an item of value, something to be remembered and cherished. I probably should have asked more. (And I wonder, today, if he had a camera hidden behind the mirror wall?)

Money has always had a secondary place in my life. Money is only a means to an end; being wealthy allows you the privilege of not worrying about the mundane, day-to-day problems that poor people have to deal with, but it doesn't guarantee you any form of actual happiness. I've always felt that those poor, deprived third-world people who are always held up as an image of poverty are probably a good deal happier in their poverty than we are, as a culture, in our relative wealth. True, their lives are shorter, but I've long since stopped including that factor in the equation. My life will probably not set any longevity records, but it's been one of the happiest, most interesting lives I've known. Would it have been different if I'd been raised in poverty, or if I'd run away and hit the streets hustling at age fifteen after spending the summer in France?

(The morning I was catching the plane home, at the end of that summer, I seriously contemplated the option of missing the plane, just losing myself on the streets of Paris, selling my body. I liked the idea, I knew I could do it, I was an adolescent queerboy in search of all the sex I could find—but it scared me, too. Hell, I'd only lost my virginity three months before! I took the safe way out. Most people think I made the right choice. I sometimes wonder.) But the thing about money that most people seem to miss is that it only does you any good if you use it. When men use it to buy sex, that's a valid expression of their values. When they use it to buy a house, or car, or a gourmet meal, ditto. When it's put in a savings account, ditto. But too many of the men who are working their asses off—and I'm talking about corporate work, here, not streetwork—don't seem to see it as a means to an end. "If I make enough money, then I'll be happy" is pure insanity . . . about as successful a strategy as "If I have enough sex, then I'll be sated." Neither commodity is evil, but neither works like a gas tank. You can't "fill up." The delightful aspect of prostitution is that it allows those people who have an excess of one commodity to exchange it for the one that they're lacking. That's what the free market is all about.

That pretty much sums up my attitude toward work of any sort. If you're doing it just for the money, you're in the wrong line of work. Oh, sure, everyone needs money to eat. But there are enough occupations in this world, people get paid for enough bizarre types of stuff, that everyone should be able to find a job that actually gives him pleasure, as well as paying the bills. (Some places, I'm told, people even get paid for writing!) In my ideal world, I have to say, sex-work as a full-time profession would not be an option for most people, simply because there would be so many part-timers doing "freelance." Oh, I'm sure there would still be openings for those with special talents—with my ability to suck my own dick, I probably would still be a curiosity, and people would pay to watch me do it—but if prostitution were de-stigmatized, I think your average housewife or construction worker would probably want to try it out on the weekends. As the supply increases, the demand decreases, until a balance is reached. If the population were genetically re-engineered so that 90 percent of all dicks were twelve inches or larger, I suspect that a six-inch dick would suddenly become the envy of everyone. (That, and we'd all have to start wearing iron underwear.) So, from a prostitute's point of view, thank god for prohibition! It's what pays the bills for many a marginal hustler: The ones who, from a rational perspective, don't have anything special in the sexual marketplace. What they're selling isn't, strictly speaking, their bodies, but their willingness to flout convention, to risk arrest and social opprobrium, and the potential subsequent reduction of their value on other job markets.

All of which may seem like it's getting excessively theoretical to those of you who just want to read about what I actually did with those few clients. Oh, get over it.

What caused me to go out in search of money in exchange for sex? Was I an emotionally-starved child, in need of ego-strokes and attention? Maybe. Yawn. I don't care what psychological motivations you want to ascribe to my performances; I was up on stage, being admired and envied and jerked off over by dozens of men nightly. Money can't buy that. Oh, maybe Bill Gates, with all his billions, could hire an auditorium full of men to worship him nightly, but I doubt that it would be the same. What made it special for me was the knowledge that these men were actually paying good money to watch me (and to top it off, they were giving me a show that I'd been known to pay money to see at various jackoff clubs around town!). That demonstrated to me just how they really felt about me; the pocketbook doesn't lie. They weren't doing it because I was buying them dinner. Money for sex is a very honest relationship: No one's trying to mislead anyone else. And that, in my book, makes it pretty special. Honesty is a rare enough commodity; combine it with pleasure, and I think you've got a working definition of Love.

I Know It When I See It

I've never pretended to be a great judge of art. When I make an excursion to an art museum—and it doesn't happen very often—it's usually for a specific purpose, to see a particular exhibit that interests me. Sometimes I'll catch something by accident, like a couple of years ago when I was in New York and was advised that I ought to go see the Gauguin show at the Met. I went, but it turned out to be one syllable off. Van Gogh, not Gauguin. Close enough.

Still, I don't see what makes these guys worth millions. Their paintings are interesting, sure, but I wouldn't hang any of them in my apartment.

What do I hang in my apartment? Used to be, my walls were crowded with dicks. I bought just about everything I could lay my hands on, for several years: Everything with any sort of erotic content. I had a pretty liberal definition of "erotic," too. Most anything can be erotic. One of my favorite pieces was a Macy's ad of a guy in construction-worker drag, with tool belt, denim shirt, hard hat—ooh, it was sexy. And a lopsided smile on his face that said, C'mon over here and get it. That was erotic. Of course, it was meant to be; we all know that sex sells. But he wasn't naked or anything; fully dressed, in fact. Everything was implied, which was the whole point. Implied sexuality can often be a lot more erotic than explicit.

A little farther down that road is the Hans-Heinrich Salmon drawing that I purchased—one of the first things I bought, in fact, back in 1984. It's a side view of a man wearing leather pants, leather cap, leather armband, and leather gloves. His arms are positioned in a bodybuilder pose, and there is very little reality to the piece. Stylized. Fetishism carried to a fine art. I just call it "Gloves" because the gloves are clearly the focus of the piece.

Another odd piece, which I bought at an auction for $60, was a large monochrome lithograph of two men fucking, face to face, with an arch in the background. It's all quite vague, and most of the lines are open to interpretation. I interpreted the arch as a stained-glass window. Some faces are visible at the top, though obscured by other details: A bearded man, and a young woman holding a baby. They're looking down at the men fucking—and smiling. The most striking thing about this piece, though, was one of the feet of the man being fucked. His feet were thrown up over the other man's shoulders, and one of them was the closest part of the work to the viewer; it was rendered quite precisely, more so than any other detail. I got the impression that the artist—and I was never sure of the signature, but I think it was Thomas C. Hinde—had more than a passing interest in feet as erotic objects. Anyway, he certainly made those toes look lickable.

The first pieces I bought, in the spring of 1984, were three panels from the Liberty Baths. This was the period in San Francisco when baths were closing left and right, and the owners of the Liberty could tell which way the wind was blowing. They decided to close, and to auction off everything, down to and including the walls. Having spent a lot of time there over the previous couple of years, I showed up for sentimental reasons—and I walked home with three huge murals, painted on particle board. Where do you put paintings of that size? Well, they took up a lot of room. One was a cowboy sitting on a fence, which I mentally christened "Cowboy about to be circumcised by his spur." Another was of two guys sucking each other off. The third was a detail copied from some Renaissance fresco, I can never remember which one. All quite gorgeous. You see, the Liberty had employed an artist-in-residence for a couple of years: David Ross, who'd pretty much lived there. He'd move into a room, cover it with murals, then move on to the next one. The murals were one of the features that I'd always loved about the place, and I was thrilled to have them in my own apartment.

What thrilled me even more was that David was there to sign all his work. An unassuming guy, not someone who you'd immediately associate with pornography. We exchanged numbers, and kept in touch. In time, we got to be good friends. He even started a sketch group, which met at my apartment for a time; I loved being able to watch all the different artists' interpretations of the models.

The evidence is anecdotal, but you're beginning to get the idea: I was pretty devoted to the promotion of Porn As Art. In fact, I began to identify the one with the other. At first, I refused to define either one. The one was "I know it when I see it," the other was "I know what I like." After a while, they blended together: Art is what gives me a hard-on, Porn is what communicates to the viewer. I'm still not quite sure that a distinction is possible or healthy, and it didn't seem useful to me. I knew what my function was: To encourage enthusiasts in both genres to forget their fear of being confused with each other. I promoted porn, but collected art; I loved art, but respected porn. Something like that.

Part of my campaign, in addition to collecting as many different artists as possible, was to model for them all. Mostly photographers: There isn't quite as much potential for sitting for painters, since that's a lot more labor-intensive. I was photographed by dozens of photographers over the years, and only sat for about five different painters (plus the members of the sketch group, which still meets; some of those sketches are quite beautiful, but none of them took more than thirty minutes). David Ross, Philip Core, Don Bachardy . . . some other artists worked from photos, which is of course a lot easier on the model, but yields a less satisfying portrait. I generally didn't ask for payment per se; I just asked for a couple of prints of their favorite photos from the session. As a result, the changes in my appearance—and there were many, over the past fourteen years—are nearly as well-documented as Princess Diana's. (I don't believe, however, that she was ever photographed with a hard-on.) Perhaps it's a sign of vanity, but I do enjoy having this historical record—especially of the times when I was enfeebled, laid low by lymphoma . . . and my subsequent return from the tomb.

Meeting Philip Core was one of the high points of my career. He was at least as fascinated by my work as I was by his; we were symbiotes, you might say. He photographed and painted me end-lessly, and produced a number of paintings—twelve that I know of, plus one larger-than-life-size sculpture—of me. I was in awe of his technique. He never achieved any great degree of recognition, in part because of the pornographic nature of much of his work. In one of his shows, when he exhibited the sculpture that he'd done of me, the dick (which was detachable) mysteriously disappeared. He and I had a good giggle over that, though it wasn't clear whether it was the curator of the gallery, a local bluenose, or an admiring visitor who had removed it.

By the time I left San Francisco, in 1988, I'd amassed a rather unwieldy collection: Some 300 pieces, many of them quite large. All the big names: Tom of Finland of course, and also Rex, Etienne, The Hun, Domino, Aries, Irizarry, Olaf, Brad Parker, Bastille, R.A. Schultz and Nigel Kent. Also photographers: Mark I. Chester in particular, but also Howard Roffman, Stanley Stellar, Jock Sturges, Joe Ziolkowski, Arthur Tress, David Lebe . . . well, like I say, I was obsessive. And my tastes were eclectic. My goal, from the beginning, was to establish a museum of erotic art—I preferred the epithet "Porn-Art"—so that these pieces would be permanently preserved. It was extremely painful to me to hear of the wanton destruction carried out by the family of one porn-art collector who died unexpectedly. Priceless, irreplaceable works by many of the above-named artists, thrown in the trash because they were "filthy."

And that's been the prevailing attitude toward this work. It's "just pornography," and not worthy of any sort of respect. With the recognition afforded to our best known artist, Tom of Finland, this has changed a bit, but most people still don't want to hang this sort of art in their living rooms. After all, the in-laws might drop in for tea . . . and that's the attitude I'm fighting. Okay, class, one more time: There is Nothing Wrong With Sex. Sex is Natural. And depicting sex, whether on canvas or in a novel or a video, is nothing more than an attempt to communicate how you feel about an aspect of your life that brings you inestimable pleasure. This is not something of which anyone should be ashamed.

I never got my museum set up. I trifled with the idea of applying for nonprofit status, but the fact is, that requires paperwork, and forms, and fundraising, and headaches, and I realized I wasn't capable of doing any of that. Instead, when the collection grew too large for me to realistically maintain it, I donated the whole thing, lock, stock, and barrel, to the Tom of Finland Foundation. They'd already jumped through all the legal hoops, and had their nonprofit status comfortably in hand. They had a board of directors who were committed to all the same things I was. And they were in Los Angeles, which was really a more appropriate place than Wisconsin for such a museum. After getting rid of the burden, I realized that it had begun weighing heavily on me: I really don't like carrying that much responsibility. Now the artwork is kept in temperature-controlled storage units, and at least a couple of times a year, portions of the collection are taken out and shown. Eventually, there will be a permanent museum where it can be on display to the public: I hope that I'm alive to see it. Partly because of this donation (though it's a change they'd already begun), the Foundation has broadened its focus beyond Tom of Finland—not just gay art, I should point out, but anything that the curator deems to be erotic. They've got lots of stuff that I would never have bought; some work that frankly repulses me. But that's okay. Hey, I don't "get" a lot of art.

I am occasionally asked to name my "favorite" artist. Can't do it. There are just too many. The piece I owned by Bastille was certainly the greatest treasure of my collection, largely because he worked in egg tempera, a very demanding medium, and produced only about forty works, I'm told, in his entire life. Mine was among the mildest: A depiction of two gas jockeys jerking each other off, it was called "L'Atelier." I never grew tired of looking at it; it seemed to glow from within. Many of his other paintings, however, were concerned with scat, a subject that does not fascinate me at all; I would not have wanted to have one of those hanging on my wall. Philip Core is the painter I most admire (and I think I owned eighteen of his pieces), but his scenes, no matter how beautiful and vivid and real they were, did not depict my jack-off fantasies. They were merely breathtaking art, which happened to include sexuality as an integral component. Mark I. Chester is a photographer (he prefers the term "iconographer") who records faithfully his subjects' fetishes, and records them in a way that the viewer can't help but feel their passion. But again, I think I'd have a hard time jerking off to most of his photos. Etienne, Domino, Rex, and Ken Wood (a relatively unknown artist who I met in 1981) were the four artists in my collection who consistently inspired me to spontaneous hard-ons. Myles Antony is another in that genre: Lushly painted water-colors of innocent youths and sleazy leathermen, tantalizingly available. Then there's Mark . . .

Mark was an artist who was represented by the RoB Gallery in Amsterdam, back before Desmodus took it over. The original owner, Rob, was a cagey fellow who never liked to share his sources, but he had work from just about every artist I've mentioned above, and a hundred others. I bought lots of my best pieces from him. And he refused to reveal who or where the artists were. Mark, he said, was an English artist, an illustrator of children's books by trade. The three pieces of his that I bought, however, were anything but child-like. They were three views of the same fantasy man: Slack-jawed, covered in black hair, jerking off, at climax, with cum gushing every which way. Enormous dick, of course, but rendered so realistically that you'd swear it was real. One of those pieces hung on my wall almost continuously from the time I bought it until I finally gave it up to the Foundation, and every visitor who saw it went weak-kneed at the sight. Most of them asked, after getting a voice back, "Is this . . . a *real* guy?"

. . . which pretty much sums up my view of what "Porn-Art" is and should be. It's what makes your knees go weak, your mouth water, your mind start racing, and your dick start stiffening. It serves as inspiration, but also as communication. No different, in fact, from any other great art. Different people give different reasons for why we have Art. I say we have it because an artist sees (or imagines) something that he thinks is so beautiful that it hurts him to think of keeping it all to himself. Some things simply have to be shared, they're too much for one person to hold. Art is our effort to share beauty. And Porn is just an effort to share sex. No difference, really. The only question is: Is it Good Art, or Bad Art? Which is to say: Does it succeed in communicating? Then, once you've settled that question, you can get down to the minor details . . . such as, Do I Like It? or Would I Have It Hanging in My House?

A few years ago, as his way of saying "Thank you" for all my support over the years, Mark I. Chester mounted a show of paintings and photographs of me. He contacted some twenty different artists, and got pieces from most of them; he even included a light-box that had 3-D slides in it, taken by my friend Kerry. (The slides were taken on a hillside near Port Angeles, Washington; with wildflowers in the foreground and the Strait of Juan de Fuca and the Olympic Mountains in the background, I felt totally at ease and in my element, and leaning over to suck my dick has never been so easy. The visitors to the show seemed to like the display, too.) I don't think I have ever been so moved by a gesture of friendship.

Seeing all these photos and paintings of me in one place made it blindingly clear to me how much I was loved, and it was simply overwhelming. Mark also set up a video camera in his spare bedroom, and invited guests on the opening night of the show to go in there and videotape a statement to me. When I got the tape, a month later, I cried. It was the most intensely emotional gift I've ever received. True, I'd spent the past decade doing my best to promote Porn Art, but I don't think it had ever occurred to me how much my efforts had been appreciated. You don't often get to hear accolades like this; they usually come posthumously. I'm very grateful to Mark for that.

As I write this, there is a controversy raging in San Francisco over a photograph of Aiden Shaw, taken by Pierre et Gilles, in which Aiden is lounging on a pile of stuffed animals, wearing cowboy boots and hat, with a semi-tumescent dick slung over his left thigh. (It's a very large dick, for those of you unfamiliar with it.) He's staring earnestly, tauntingly, at the camera. This photo has raised such a ruckus because it was used on a flyer promoting the Sex Ball—a dance party—and flyers were distributed in relatively public places in the Castro. The editor of one of "our" newspapers wrote a very stuffy editorial proclaiming that such photos had no place in public life, declaring haughtily that gay men should keep themselves covered and stop flaunting their sexuality. This controversy will blow over in time, probably within a few weeks; either the editor will be fired (one can only hope) or people will forget about it. But it outlines my struggle in the clearest possible terms. On the one side are the people who believe that dicks, and indeed anything that might incite people to lascivious thoughts, should be kept securely out of sight, and we should only undress in our bedrooms, with the lights out; on the other side are the people who believe that the human body is a work of art, and should be appreciated, everywhere, at all times. Aiden Shaw is most emphatically a work of art, and the photo in question does nothing but add to his allure and expressiveness. This is a photo, in fact, that speaks to me . . . and I think it ought to be on every streetcorner in America. It says, in one photo, everything one really needs to say about porn, art, sex, and communication. True, I don't know much about Art . . . but I know it when I see it.

You May Already Be Dead

Today I saw the doctors. Not a pastime I can recommend,
though popular as hell these days. It seems my friends
would rather do their cruising in an institution
than a bar—the lighting's better, smoking's not allowed,
and—is there a subtle way to say this?—you meet a better crowd.
These men look up, when I walk in; they smile in recognition,
or simple comradeship. And no, I haven't taken any of them home,
to date; but there's a look we share, that says, We All Are Dying—
And So What? Each morning, as I do my day's ablution,
I study carefully my face. Is this the countenance of coming death?
Well, yes, it is. The knowledge, though, does not prevent my smiling
at the strangers met in grocery stores, while walking through the
    Mission,
or in coffeeshops. So many seem afraid to meet my gaze . . .
reminding me that life itself is just a passing phase.

November 20, 1996

. . . And Never Simple

Telling the truth is a funny thing. Truth is a rare commodity in our society, feared and hated by many, simply discounted as irrelevant by others. I've spent a lot of time, the past six months, hanging around with a group of people for whom truth is a lifeline: Addicts in recovery. One of the basic principles that keeps us clean and sober is honesty. Not just honesty about drugs; honesty about everything.

Have you noticed that life seldom follows a predictable path? Sometimes it seems that there's no path at all, that it just disappears in the woods . . . and then suddenly you're on a new path, one that you never anticipated, but suddenly you're running full tilt down it, eagerly looking forward to the next adventure . . . and you run right off the edge of a cliff, and hang there, like Wile E. Coyote, legs working furiously for a minute or two before noticing that you're unsupported. Okay, it only seems that way. But that's what I'm doing: Trying to make sense of a life that seems, from all perspectives, perfectly improbable. That's what one reviewer wrote about my last book: That he found some sections "difficult to believe." You and me both, honey. The thing is, though, life itself is simple. You just live. It's the interpretation of it, the making sense of it, the conscious effort to force yourself to tell the truth, that's complicated. Society really doesn't support honesty, no matter how much it professes to. (Think about it.) Most people would rather hear a comfortable lie than the uncomfortable truth.

There's just one thing the truth has going for it. It may not be easy, or simple . . . but it can be a helluva lot of fun. Trust me.

Taking Photos

There was a time when photographs were not essential: When we were all still immortal, when the need to preserve each face on celluloid or videotape was not felt so urgently. That was the time when I met Martin. It wasn't happenstance. I sought him out: I'd been told that some faggots lived at this particular address, and I wanted to get to know them, as carnally as possible. So no, I wasn't looking for Martin in particular, but he was the first one I saw, and I thought he'd do just fine.

I don't often think of him, nowadays. He's been dead for ten years: One of the fairly early AIDS casualties. But it doesn't take much to bring back the unique sound of his laughter, or the way his lower lip hung down, almost pouting, but in a way that always kept me wondering whether or not he was putting me on. Detecting irony has never been my strong suit. And then there's that smell . . .

To the best of my knowledge, at that point in my life, I'd only met one faggot—and he'd taught me some of the rudiments of how to behave, sexually, but I still felt totally innocent and vulnerable. I didn't know what to expect when Martin came out to greet me. There was no one else in sight. He was wearing shorts. I introduced myself and stuck out my hand; he ignored it, walked right up to me, and hugged me. Surprised the hell outta me.

In retrospect, I find it incredible that he would do that. Wonderful, but incredible. I mean, it was obvious that I was underage, and I know Martin wasn't a chicken hawk. He hugged me because he could tell that I was nervous as a cat, and he thought that would calm me down. It did. Took a while before I stopped shaking, but when I did, I was in love. With the first man in my life who'd ever just walked up to me and hugged me. In love—and intensely aware of the intoxicating smell that emanated from him.

We went back into the house, and talked for a while, and maybe we had some tea, I don't know. Then—"I've got to get back to work weeding the garden. Would you like to help?" Now, it's funny: Weeding my family's garden had never been one of my favorite activities, but the idea of working a hoe while standing next to Martin, well, it made funny little ripples go up and down my stomach.

June in Southern Oregon. I've avoided it ever since then. I'll go back for a visit in spring or fall, but the dry heat, the fields that turn golden brown and prickly, the burrs that stick to you if you brush against any plant, not to mention the hay fever that started to afflict me every year about that time—it makes me look back at Oregon with something slightly less than nostalgia. This particular day—well, okay, it wasn't quite June yet. It was the last weekend in May, but it was blazing hot. That much I remember. Not exactly a photograph, but a sensory impression. Perhaps if I had been able to spend that summer doing nothing but tending the garden in the burning sun with Martin at my side, I would've grown to love hot weather. I remember working, talking, and every now and then, when a slight breeze would come by, I could smell Martin's sweat—one of the strongest sweat smells I'd ever encountered, it was sweet, and spicy, and powerfully erotic to me. Had I ever given thought to sweat as an aphrodisiac? I'm not even sure. I know it didn't take me long to make the connection.

With four hands . . . well, it wasn't a big garden. We finished in under an hour, and a good thing, too, because the day had gotten quite unbearably hot out in the sun. Martin suggested a swim in the creek, and I enthusiastically agreed. Then, as I passed him, going back to the house, he put his arm around my shoulder, pulled me to a stop, and said, "Come here." And this time it wasn't "just" a hug: He kissed me, using those wonderful lips to full advantage, softening and opening, teaching me the sensuality of mouths—all while I was hyperventilating, of course, and the smell of his sweat, dripping from his armpits, was making my head spin like a top. And his hands were holding me tight to keep me from slipping to the ground.

Several minutes later: "Now, let's take that swim."

I think of Martin every time I read a news item about some poor boy being "molested." I was molested that afternoon, no question of it. Molested in the way every adolescent boy should be molested, if our society weren't so pathologically afraid of sex. Martin took me down to the creek, which was ice-cold and felt marvelous, and we frolicked in the pool for a few minutes. Then we began caressing each other, still waist-deep in the water. Eventually we made it out onto one of the sunwarmed boulders next to the stream. Memory may iron out a few of the kinks; I'm sure that it wasn't all as idyllic and seamless as my mind would like to tell me. The rock that we lay on probably wasn't smooth, there were undoubtedly mosquitoes, and I've no doubt that when he first started to fuck me, it hurt. But I don't remember those things. What I remember is his kisses, and the fact that he fucked me, and came in me, and looked in my eyes afterward and laughed, softly, that heart-melting laugh of his, and I felt loved.

I would have liked to have fallen in love with Martin. That is, I tried pretty damn hard to get him to fall in love with me. Never a good strategy. Trying too hard is almost always counterproductive. I saw him a couple more times that summer, and had sex at least once more (strange that I can't remember exactly how many times!), but then, sometime before summer's end, he had the good taste to take me aside and explain some things to me. Like: Yes, he liked me, but he'd also like to avoid being lynched by the townsfolk, so could I please cool it, huh? I was crushed, but I tried to take it in stride. I went off in search of new dick.

I never took any photos of Martin. Photos, for some strange reason, are something that you most often take of people younger than yourself. Perhaps it's a mystical attempt to recapture their youth. Martin was thirteen years older than I, an adult, and I worshipped him, but I wouldn't have thought to photograph him even if I'd had a camera, which I didn't. When I next saw him, several years later, our respective status had equaled somewhat; the passage of time will do that. His eyes were still as seductive as ever, and the scent of his armpits was still my ideal aphrodisiac.

And so his memory fades, slowly. He was never a major part of my life, however much I would've liked him to be, and he was one more member of that legion of men who died without my ever knowing they were sick. Just the simplest of obituaries, and a sick pain inside me, wishing that I'd managed to see more of him. Not to "say goodbye," exactly, but to spend time with him, to kiss him, to be fucked by him again—to let him know that he was loved. That's what I wish I'd been able to do.

Today, going through stacks of old newspapers (yes, I am a hoarder), I found one from 1984: A cover photograph of Martin and another man, in a play. The other man is also dead, now; he's someone else who I worshipped, though less intimately. Finding these photos of dead friends, as I continue to do, almost every time I turn around . . . well, it's sad, of course. At the same time that it reminds me of the person, it reminds me of how little I knew of him. I didn't see Martin in the play that he was photographed in, though I did see him in others: I always felt a vicarious thrill of pride at the thought that I "knew" that man up on stage, knew him in a special, intimate way.

That's what sex seemed like when I was twenty. I had not yet come to the amusing realization that yes, sex is special and intimate, but that Martin had probably been specially intimate with half the male members of the audience, and I could get over my sense of uniqueness.

After the swim, and the sex, and probably a spot of lunch with the other household members . . . well, I don't remember, but I probably didn't stick around much longer. Had to get back home. So I floated back across the footbridge, back into the real world, looking upstream, as I crossed, at that magical pool that was already entering my personal mythology. And Memorial Day Weekend was just beginning.

Neither the house nor the footbridge exist anymore; one was destroyed by fire, one by flood. My mental images are quite inaccurate, I'm sure. It might be nice to have a photo of them. It would be even nicer if I'd taken a photo of that sunwarmed rock: The last time I visited the place, I couldn't remember which one it was. None of them looked very comfortable, but that might just be due to my advancing years. The young are so flexible, so hardy. So impressionable. To this day, I have yet to meet a man with the same heavenly pit smell as Martin, but I'm still looking.

Turned Off

I would now like to expound, at length, on a subject of which I am wholly ignorant—or at least, that I've done my level best, over the years, to remain oblivious to. In this screed I will probably bear an uncanny resemblance to many of our most famous televangelists, who talk endlessly of places they've never been and people they've never met . . . but sometimes observation is as useful a tool as experience, and I've certainly observed how this subject has affected the world around me. I'm talking about television.

I grew up almost entirely deprived of the influence of television; except for the occasional sleepover at some friend's house, I never got to watch it. This bothered me at the time. In college, even though there was a set in the common room of the dorm, I rarely went down there; I was busy all the time. The next two years were spent hopping from place to place, and large acquisitions were out of the question. It wasn't until 1982 that I succumbed.

Curiously enough, I bought my first VCR and camcorder—a Betamax—before buying a TV. Makes sense, from a certain perspective. I didn't necessarily want to *watch* myself on TV, but I did want my various "looks" preserved for posterity. Soon enough, though, I did buy a monitor, and although it spent a couple of years in storage, I kept it up until 1987, when I hit the road again, eventually settling in Wisconsin. For much of the nineties—1991 to 1997—I did again own a TV monitor, but no antenna; it was strictly for watching porn videos. And then, early this year, I realized that I wasn't even using it for that anymore, so I decided to get rid of it. Haven't missed it, so far.

During those periods of being "plugged in," yes, I did have my addictions. Mostly PBS, of course—you would expect anything else of me?—but there was a period, I remember, when I tried to watch *Donahue* every afternoon. (Now, Scott, is such honesty *really* necessary? I mean, some of our readers have heart conditions. . . .)

Am I richer for any of this couch surfing? No, frankly, I don't think so. Despite all the arguments from advocates of public television, despite all my friends' glowing descriptions of their favorite shows, my assessment is that absolutely *anything* I could have been doing during those hours—bicycling in the park, doing my laundry, jerking off, reading, eating, or doing crossword puzzles—would have enriched my life more than sitting and absorbing cathode rays. There. That's a fairly damning statement. If I am ever reduced to a state where watching TV is the most productive thing I can do, I hope someone will have the mercy to euthanize me.

Still, I hear a lot of you ask: What about porno? Don't you miss watching it? After all, it was my career for five years, and I've remained a staunch supporter of it in the years since then. I still support the absolute right of filmmakers, writers, photographers, and artists of all sorts to produce whatever the hell turns them on. I give no credence whatsoever to the feminist critique of porn as "violence against women"; I know from personal experience that all the concern about porn actors being "exploited" is so much bushwah, and I believe children are harmed more by overprotective parents who try to shield them from the realities of the world than they could possibly be by the sight of two naked people having sex. (In my ideal world, porn tapes would be part of the normal school curriculum, from kindergarten on up—and kids' reactions would be "so what's the big deal?") All that having been said . . . watching porn tapes bores me to tears, now, and I hope I never have to see another one. This isn't all about their quality (although it's true that ninety percent of them are pretty fucking lousy); it mostly has to do with the attitude that goes into making them. You see, I have this quaint notion that people should enjoy what they do for a living: "If it doesn't give you pleasure, you're in the wrong line of work" has always been my motto. I have very little sympathy for people who bitch and moan about their jobs. They've made a choice (which they're free to un-make at any time—indentured servitude was outlawed some years ago in this country). And the people in these videos—even though they're having sex, and moaning in presumed ecstasy—don't appear to be having a good time. It depresses me to watch most of them, because they look like they lead such wretchedly unhappy and joyless lives that I wonder they don't attempt

suicide more often than they do. If I didn't know better, I might
think these really were boys who had been kidnapped and forced to
perform at gunpoint. Sex, for me, is joyful, friendly, and intimate—
or it is nothing. And the sex portrayed in most videos is nothing.

With a couple of notable exceptions, I had fun making porn. I got
along with the directors, with my co-stars, with the tech crews; I
loved being "a cast member." (No, no one ever did cast my member. Though I did have at least one offer. I frankly didn't think I
could maintain a hard-on long enough for a decent reproduction.)
So the boredom and contempt I see written all over the faces of our
current crop of pornstars puzzles me. Can working conditions have
changed so drastically in ten years? I think not. Does AIDS, and the
acceptance of condoms on set, contribute to it? Is it due to the
reliance on "straightboys" for the talent pool? Could it be attributable to the emphasis on the three Bs (buff, beautiful, and brainless)?
Is it all a matter of what gay men today are looking for, as most
directors will allege? I find all these explanations hard to believe,
and I end up by tracing the problem back to its source. If porno
weren't such a stigmatized medium—if it were sold above ground,
without social opprobrium or fear of legal persecution—I'm confident that we could develop a real exchange of ideas between producers and consumers. The audience would feel free to ask for what
they want, and the producers wouldn't be afraid to portray it. Then
we might see some masterpieces in the genre again, like the Gage
Brothers films of the seventies. But what I'm talking about, here, is
a total realignment of government and society, a fundamental recognition that sex is not the enemy and prohibition is never the
answer. And I'm not optimistic.

Where was I? Oh, that's right, talking about television. Or, more
precisely, why I'm turned off by television. I don't think I need to
add more words to the reams of criticism that the medium has
already received; I'll just say that there are few things that I find
more insulting than to go home with a man and have him turn on the
TV the minute we walk in the door. There's a message there, which
I don't think I need to spell out to you, and my usual response is,
"Excuse me, I think I've made a mistake, good night."

I'll add one more anecdote, representative of my relationship
with The Box. Several summers ago, a friend of mine organized a

trip to San Miguel de Allende, Mexico, to view the total solar eclipse. There were four of us; we arrived a couple of days early, and spent the time exploring the town. It's a lovely place: Touristy, yes, but not spoiled. That is to say, the townsfolk don't all work for tour agencies and hotels. There is "real life." I even managed a sexual encounter with a local: He took me back to his apartment, telling me his wife was away for the week visiting her family. (I was rather proud of myself for this escapade, since I've never been very good at navigating the straits of repression.) Then, on eclipse day, we all drove about an hour south of town and climbed a hill in the middle of nowhere. The eclipse was pretty spectacular, I grant you, and we all took our clothes off and capered about like fools and took lots of photos. I'd been a bit cynical about the whole event, to begin with: Yeah, sure, the sun's going away, it's going to get dark, whoopee. This happens nightly, doesn't it? But to my surprise, I found it strangely exciting, in ways I can't quite describe. I think it had a lot to do with our remote location, the elevation, and the fact that the clouds broke just before the eclipse. It's always impressive when Mother Nature cooperates so splendidly.

That night, driving back north, we stopped in Ciudad Victoria, on the Gulf Coast. We got up to our hotel room . . . and what did my companions do but turn on the TV to watch the news coverage of the eclipse. I couldn't believe it. Here we'd just witnessed something truly spectacular, in person, under the best possible conditions . . . and they needed to see it on TV, to "prove" to themselves that it actually happened. They kept watching the various newscasts long after I'd crawled into bed. I lay there, incredulous. At midnight, when the TV turned to white noise, and no one turned it off, I realized that they'd all fallen asleep. Seething, I got up and went out. I spent the next six hours walking around the town, trying to tire myself out and dissipate my anger. I don't like being angry. But I felt like they'd taken something special, something real, and turned it into a tawdry imitation of life: Life as interpreted by newscasters and talk show hosts. And I realized that I never again wanted to be alone with someone who thought that TV was more interesting than real life.

They say that man is an inherently social animal. I sometimes wonder if I'm fully human, because all other things being equal, most times I'd rather be by myself than with anyone I can name. I can think more clearly, accomplish more, focus on whatever it is I'm doing—even if I'm only listening to music, I find it dreadfully annoying to have someone in the room trying to make conversation—and have a more satisfying orgasm by myself than with anyone else. I am driven outside of myself mostly by the desire to be touched, to be held . . . which definitely *is* a universal human need. At those moments when that urge becomes irresistible, I used to make a dash for the nearest bathhouse. Whether or not I ended up bathed in cum, I knew there would be people there who were looking for more or less the same thing I was, and friendly, relaxed conversation was usually available. Nowadays, I call up my boyfriend, and we have lunch. In either case, however, it's interaction with real people, instead of flickering phantasms on a cathode-ray tube.

It's that boyfriend, though, who finally moved me to get rid of the TV that I'd hauled with me back from my isolation in Wisconsin. There, okay, it served a purpose; porn videos, stale as they were, did at least provide some entertainment on long winter nights. Here in San Francisco, there's really no excuse for it. Something is happening, every minute of every day, that is more worthwhile than watching a video; I can't possibly take in all of it. And all through this last spring, Chris would regularly come over to my place with a couple of videos he'd rented, and wheedle me into watching them with him. I was in love; I was malleable. But it annoyed the hell out of me (and I don't *like* being annoyed with someone I'm in love with, dammit!) and after a few months I decided the only solution was to get rid of the TV and VCR entirely. I didn't want to have them in the apartment any more, didn't want them to ever be the reason Chris came over to visit. The video collection has been somewhat slower to go: I had hundreds of tapes, accumulated over sixteen years, and many of them had particular sentimental value— mostly, as records of friends who are now dead. Chris Burns, Jon King, Tony Bravo, Rydar Hanson, and many more. But they've been winnowed down considerably now. Writing about them makes it easier to discard the artifacts; they're properly memorialized.

It's arguable that I was "addicted" to porno. I certainly spent a lot more time and money on that collection than was healthy or sane (including thousands of magazines and books, too, not just videos); and it definitely got in the way of my "real" life. You know: writing, gardening, sleeping, eating, working. The only problem with using that term is that addiction isn't something that just disappears, and today, I feel no desire for porn. I'm still on all the mail order companies' mailing lists, and I get their brochures and glance over them . . . and giggle. Oh, of course I appreciate the photos of all those buff guys in butch poses, but mostly they just make me depressed. I don't want that in my life. I've got something better. At least, that's the way it seems to me now.

What I really do want to do is appear in one more porn video. I'd spend the first thirty minutes in an intricate seduction, with another average-looking guy (or guys), leading up to sex . . . and then, just as we're finally about to go at it, I'd look up at the camera and say, "Why the hell are you watching us? Why don't you go out and *get a life?*"—and I'd reach up and douse the lights. The rest of the video would be a black screen, with a realistic soundtrack of sex in the dark—that is, lots of "Oops!" and "Sorry, was that your elbow?" and "Where's the lube?" type comments. No, there's no market for it . . . besides, I have more fun writing books. And I meet a better class of people: people who don't necessarily spend their lives in front of their TVs.

Slightly More Than Two Cents Worth

I am sometimes asked, by folks unfamiliar with the industry, "But don't porn producers exploit their performers?" I never know quite where to begin with these people; they don't seem to have any concept of the term "power dynamics," at least not in a real-world sense. (Though it's true, I've seldom been accused of living in the "real world" myself.) Pornstars are getting paid relatively huge sums of money for doing practically nothing; the people who claim that they're being exploited are the same people who think that sex in general is degrading. Well, yes, if it's degrading to you, you shouldn't be in the business. But I have yet to hear one single story of a pornstar or starlet who was drugged, bound, and made to do porn against his or her will. We were in it because there were obvious rewards, whether monetary or less tangible. And as often as not, I feel that the producers are the ones who sell themselves short. Let me tell you a short story . . .

I'll start by telling the story as objectively as possible, then I'll do my judgmental best. You've been warned. I have a friend (using the term loosely: Someone I've known for a fair number of years) in the industry, who has been in a number of pornflicks. He knows his way around a porn set better than I do. Recently, he made a "spanking video" for a very small company. I don't know what all he had to do in the film, but when he mentioned it to me he didn't sound like the idea horrified him. It was just another job. He was paid $600—not a princely sum, but for a small niche-market production like this, not bad, either. There was a verbal understanding that the video would be marketed—but no written contract or model release signed.

Some time later, when my friend saw an ad for the resulting video on the Internet, he realized that he had an opportunity staring him in the face. He called a lawyer, and initiated a lawsuit against the producer, on the grounds that the video had been marketed without a model release. His name and image, he said, had been used without his permission. His lawyer, he told me in eager tones, had told him that he might expect to get "ten to fifty thousand" out of this lawsuit, if handled right, and if the producer had insurance. Otherwise, the advice was, he should drop the suit, as the company was clearly not large enough to support a judgment of that size.

So the lawyer sent the producer a letter demanding that my friend's name and likeness be removed from all advertising, videos, etc. The producer sent back a polite letter agreeing, stating that he would do his best to comply, in every particular—but adding that it would be impossible to meet the deadline set by the lawyer, since he had not received the demand until two days after said deadline.

Okay, here's where the judgmental part begins. You can stop reading if you like. Behavior like this qualifies a person for the appellation "pond scum." I don't use that term lightly. I've used it about one particular magazine editor who makes a habit of not paying writers who she's published, and I frequently use it about "parking control officers," and vice cops—sometimes about IRS agents. Welcome to the club, guy. He wanted to know my opinion: Was he likely to prevail? I told him, in the most neutral tones I could muster, that yes, I thought he was probably within the letter of the law, that what he had apparently had with the producer was something called a "gentlemen's agreement," which unfortunately was only useful when used between gentlemen. The producer had obviously not realized what sort of person he was dealing with.

You'll notice that I have very conspicuously avoided mentioning the name of this pornstar. This is for obvious reasons, since I've no wish to be on the receiving end of his second legal assault. (He very proudly prefaced this story to me with the comment, "It's my first lawsuit!") But given this sort of behavior on the part of pornstars, really, how do you expect producers to behave? I admit, this is an egregious example . . . but it's far from the only one that I've seen. In this business, more often than not, it's the producers who are sincerely trying to help their talent "get on their feet," counseling them and cutting them slack and *lending them money*, fergodsakes!—and the talent who are trying to rip off the producers for all they're worth. No, it's not universal—tell me, what statement can you make about any group of people that *is* universal?—but it's far more common than the reverse.

And here I sit, fulminating at a phenomenon that doesn't have anything to do with pornography, really, but with modern life in general. You meet up with opportunists and parasites everywhere you go. "Hey, this is my chance to get ahead!" I was told, enthusiastically, after I'd made clear my disapproval. Somehow I don't think so, but then, I'm old-fashioned. I think one is most likely to "get ahead" by being honest and straightforward with people, by behaving with something quaint known as "honor." (I'm tempted to be *really* quaint, and call it "honour," since it's apparently a concept foreign to Americans.) But no, pond scum floats to the top by using the flatulence of the legal system for buoyancy, so it has no need of honor. The laws are made for people who don't know what's honorable, or don't care, in an attempt to keep them in check. Myself, I don't much care about the laws. I've broken quite a number of them in my time, and I hope to break even more before I die. Laws give an artificial backbone to the people born without one; I'm happy to say that I don't feel the need for that moral prosthesis.

Okay, I've probably made more than a few of you puke by now with all my self-righteous moral huffing and puffing. My boyfriend looks at me when I get like this and says, in tones of something between disgust and pity, "Scott, you really think you're superior to most people, don't you?" He has this odd notion, I think, that all men are equal, that there's no point in trying to make yourself better. Yes, Chris, I do consider myself "superior to most people." Most people are unprincipled boors. These are not innate characteristics, these are things they choose to be, because it's easier, because this is the way they think they can "get ahead." I try very hard to limit my associations with those folk, because yes, I do like to be around people who believe in the power of human—not divine—redemption. We can make ourselves better . . . or we can slide down into the pond scum. It's a choice, folks. Anytime you hear someone trying to pass the buck—"oh, I'm this way because my parents abused me," or, "because my people have been oppressed for centuries," or "because I've got AIDS," or "because I grew up in poverty"—my advice is, run for the hills.

The pornstar in question, I'm happy to say, dropped his lawsuit, at least in part because of my patent disapproval. People don't often take my advice—hey, I don't often feel qualified to give it, even when asked. I know how I want to live my life, but I seldom feel like taking responsibility for anyone else's moral health. I'm not sure why I felt that this instance merited an exception . . . but I'm glad I did.

Gay Life Ends at 40

I have seven years left, I keep telling myself. Six . . . five . . . four
. . . Before I reach that dreaded age, and I have to wear my trousers
rolled. Or whatever it is gay men do of a similar vein: Hang out at
The Glass Coffin and learn to like martinis, I suppose. Begin to
frequent the tearoom at Sears, desperately hoping for some trade
who doesn't care what I look like, just wants to stick his dick
through a gloryhole and get off. Buy a miniature schnauzer to keep
myself company on those long evenings alone. Collect Wedge-
wood.

Okay, I'll lay off the stereotype. I presume it's obvious that I
don't really believe in it, that I'm writing tongue-in-cheek. (It *is*
obvious, isn't it? Please tell me it is.) Forty . . . well, there was a
time, long ago, when that age held some terror for me. Oddly
enough, it was long before I was ever exposed to gay life. When I
was about fourteen, I vividly recall a solemn vow between my best
friend and I that we were going to commit suicide on our fortieth
birthdays, that surely life wouldn't be worth living after that decrepit age. Our reasons for deciding this? I really can't remember. In
fact, it's quite puzzling, given the fact that some of the most admired people in my life—teachers and neighbors, mostly—were
quite obviously over forty, and didn't seem to be having a miserable
time of it. I think our pledge had more to do with the melodrama of
the idea. Too many readings of "To An Athlete Dying Young."
Better to burn the candle at both ends and go out in a blaze of glory.
That sort of thing.

I got over it. (Having lost touch with that friend, I'll probably
never know if he did, but I rather assume so. It's a highly romantic
notion, but a bit juvenile.) I don't remember a sudden change of
mind, but at age twenty-two or thereabouts I can remember thinking
about that pledge and being slightly horrified. Suicide? No. Life is
too good to ever consider a voluntary end. (My sister's suicide

undoubtedly helped me reach that conclusion: A senseless and sad death, with not the slightest touch of heroism or tragedy to it.) And this, despite the fact that I was well immersed in the gay culture, which at that point in time consisted almost exclusively of under-forties. I didn't give a lot of thought to the subject, but I felt confident that I would live to a happy old age, along with all those wonderful tricks, friends, lovers, fuckbuddies, sisters, soulmates, roommates, pen-pals, travel companions . . . all those wonderful gay men who had become part of my life. Most of these men were somewhat older than I; that was always my preference. Some of them were twice my age. I could see that their lives were not conforming to the stereotype. When confronted with a cliche and a reality that so obviously conflict, I tend to believe reality. These men were enjoying their lives. More to the point, I enjoyed being around them—and by extrapolation, I thought it likely that when I reached their age there would be other twenty-two-year-olds who would take pleasure in my company. (I believe I faced that thought with some terror, actually: The idea of trying to keep up with someone twenty years my junior. I've never been an athletic sort.)

In the middle of this complicated process of growing up and learning about gay life, I somehow managed to get caught up in one of the most youth-oriented professions that's ever existed: Pornography. My interaction with that world still leaves me a bit bemused. Despite having been part and parcel of it for five years, and being truly devoted to it as a career, I never became a "typical" starlet. I didn't support myself by hustling; I didn't do drugs; I didn't go out dancing; I didn't steal cars or engage in other criminal activity; and I didn't accept the West Hollywood notion that only the young and beautiful are worth fucking. I'm sorry to say that the popular stereotypes of pornstars are uncomfortably close to the truth. After all, these are juveniles we're talking about here, boys who never grew up. And I had nothing in common with them. You want to know the one person from my porn years whom I considered my closest friend? A photographer, who worked with me on several films, who was at least forty at the time. Greying beard, bearskin rug on his chest, not gym-toned, and full of sage advice for ambitious little me. Did we have sex? Not in any traditional sense, no. He had a lover, and I respected that. But I found him much more attractive and sexy than most of the twenty-year-old twinkies who were thrown at me on screen.

I wasn't making the movies, however. The men who produced them, fifty-year-olds, all of them, couldn't see the beauty and strength in a man of their own generation.

There has been some alteration in the public perception of older gay men over the past decade: The law of supply and demand, for one thing, has made them more valuable. In the leather community, the Young Turks are said to be wondering "where have all the daddies gone." And in porn flicks, we now occasionally see hot men with hairy chests and receding hairlines. Occasionally. There's a hint of hero worship in the air, a slight sense of a search for authority figures, that warms my heart and at the same time worries me. I'm not sure how accurate this notion is; it may be purely sentiment on the part of the survivors. At the very least, I've been gratified by the current fashion (which will undoubtedly be past by the time this book sees print) for shaved heads. It's not exactly a declaration of solidarity with older men, bald men, but it's an implicit welcome to them, an invitation to rejoin the community . . . and an indication that we're losing some of our fear of appearing older than we are.

Nevertheless . . . the stereotype persists. Not necessarily that life ends at forty, but that gay men over forty will never get laid again, so they'd better have something else. The two most popular options seem to be a career and a lover. Something to lessen the pain of your vanished sex life, something to give you comfort in your declining years. Now, I'm all in favor of having a consuming career, something that gives a deep sense of satisfaction (similar, yes, to the abiding bliss of being well fucked), but I know better than to think that it replaces sex. Fortunately, I know that even this watered-down version of the myth is wildly inaccurate. I know lots of old-timers who get more sex than I do. Yes, I'll freely admit that I'm getting it a lot less often than I did when I was twenty-two, but that's primarily due to my lowered libido. I can't handle a night at the baths anymore. I still go, occasionally, for a nostalgic trip down memory lane. But now I go in the afternoon, instead, and frequently find myself napping in the hot tub. And this decline in desire (and energy level) does not distress me unduly. Despite the multitude of "disasters" that have befallen me over the years, I find myself enjoying life more and more with every passing year. I think it's mainly due to a process of learning, and that's something that I don't expect to stop. So I'm convinced that, however long I live, I'll keep on enjoying life. Even if I end up blind, deaf, crippled, impotent, asthmatic . . . as long as I still have my mental faculties, the ability to learn, I bet life will still seem pretty wonderful.

And then again, I've seen some demented and/or senile guys who seemed pretty cheerful, too.

I suppose part of the credit for my attitude has to go to AIDS. As it killed off so many of my contemporaries and elders—and, now, so many younger people as well—it gave me that much more appreciation for the joys of ageing. As I mourned, as the waste of human talent became more and more appalling, I couldn't help projecting those truncated lives into the future. I knew what wonderful work Robert Chesley produced at age thirty-five. What might he have written at age seventy-five, with forty more years of experience behind him? Not a new thought, I know, but it serves as a useful counterweight to the pointless bathos of Housman's poem. I determined that I was going to make use of every minute left to me . . . and it kind of put in perspective that amusing countdown: Five . . . four . . . three. . .

Nothing could possibly make me "retire" from the company of gay men at age forty, or any other age. My friends (and virtually all my friends are gay men) are some of the liveliest and most interesting people I can imagine, and I don't think a particular birthday is liable to change them any more than it will change me. Will I grow vain (more vain) and start wearing a toupee? God, I hope not. (As sexy as I find bald and/or shaved heads, I kinda doubt it.) Will I acquire a lover, as insurance against a lonely and anxious old age? I'd rather have the toupee, thanks. There will be changes in my outlook as I age; that's a given. I'll learn new tastes, acquire new obsessions, perhaps lose my fondness for Ogden Nash or Andrea Marcovicci or fig sandwiches. Maybe even (and this is scary) my taste for Mexicans. Anything's possible. But the prospect doesn't really frighten me. Change is growth, I keep reminding myself (only slightly tongue-in-cheek), and whatever changes I undergo as the calendar flips by will be changes for the good. Progress, as Nash reminds us, is an advance toward perfection. What role will I have, as a seventy-year-old, in the gay community? (And yes, I do assume that I'll live that long.) Who knows? I think it would be lovely if I could play the part of grandfather to the young queerboys who are just learning about sex and Sondheim. Someone's got to teach them, and parents are often not prepared. (Will this change in forty years? It's too much to hope for.) Naturally, I hope that my writings will be read; I hope that my videos will still be watched, and jerked off to . . . but these hopes are based on the person I am today. My priorities will change.

There's no way to tell what will be important, to me or to gay society, in forty years. Could Harry Hay have possibly envisioned the world he'd help to create? I think not. I hope that he's happy with the result. I am. Life is good—in large part due to joyful pioneers like Harry, who didn't believe in suicide, either metaphorical or literal, at forty.

Billiard Ball

. . . as I felt his freshly-shaven head rubbing slowly, sensuously, insistently, against my well-fucked asshole, two of our bodies' most intensely erogenous zones sliding together in a frictionless dance of desire—I moaned. He began pushing his head upward more insistently; my body quivered. I could feel my ass opening, opening, opening wider than I'd ever known before—and then the smooth skin of his scalp working its way into me, in and out, in and out, a delirious reverse-childbirth that sent me spiraling off into some other reality . . .

Okay, it's a fantasy. Not reality. Don't confuse the two. As I write this, THE fashion statement of 1996 appears to be winding down. For the first time in my life, I am actually distressed to see the end of a fad. Clothing styles, language mannerisms, *Dynasty* and disco, all came and went without even registering on my cultural awareness meter. But when I moved back to San Francisco in May 1995 and saw the proliferation of naked heads, I will admit I went a little apeshit. These were the men I'd always wanted; these were the new Queer Gods. Suddenly, I felt like part of the tribe.

The first time I had my head shaved was in 1980, when I was eighteen. I rode into New Orleans (a town I'd never been to), walked into a bar dressed in my full riding leathers, and said, to the first man who expressed interest in me, the eighteen-year-old equivalent of "Do with me what you will." And he did. The next morning, stumbling out into the sunshine rubbing my gleaming scalp (and feeling my baby-smooth skin under my clothes), I felt like a new man. Or boy, if you prefer.

Later that day, I was in Biloxi. That was the point of the trip, really: visiting a high school buddy of mine who was stationed at the Air Force base there. This was a real strange experience for me. From the moment I arrived at the gate, I was treated with some peculiar combination of suspicion and awe. They didn't quite know what to make of me. I was asked by no fewer than three men (after I took off my helmet) if I'd just arrived from Basic Training. Apparently they thought that I'd been unsatisfied with the military regulation haircut, and had decided to go all the way. They almost acted afraid of me: Somewhere between, "This guy's *real* butch" and "This guy's a rebel." I'd never gotten that reaction from straight men (okay, boys) before; in high school, I was the nerd. It was a thrill, but I have to admit I didn't understand why a haircut should make such a difference.

Over the next fifteen years, I shaved my head (or let someone else shave it) dozens of times. I seldom kept it that way for long; it takes too much work to keep it smooth. While living in Hawaii in 1982, I maintained it for a while, but I grew irritated with all my friends who insisted on calling me Mr. Clean—not my favorite nickname. (Cleanliness is next to godliness in my book, and I'm not much interested in faith and charity, either.) I don't think I've ever said "No" to any top who told me he was going to shave me. (If he made the mistake of *asking*, on the other hand . . .) Hair grows back, you know? And if it gives you a thrill, why not? Then there was the six-month period in 1993-1994 when I was undergoing chemotherapy: I lost every hair on my body, right down to my eyebrows, and it was heaven. I fantasized about continuing what I called "cosmetic chemo" indefinitely. Not practical, alas.

The fantasy with which I started this piece belongs, I'm sorry to say, in the same category as my fantasies about centaurs and satyrs: Unlikely to transpire in this world. As an actual act, I'm not sure I'd even want it. It's the idea that is so stimulating. Two of the body's most sensitive patches of skin, rubbing against each other. Oh, I've done the preliminaries with lots of guys: brushing my head lightly against his perineum, spreading wide his buttcheeks and rubbing his asshole over as many square inches of naked scalp as possible, getting more forceful and butting his butt like a billygoat. It's very sexy. On the couple of occasions when I've tried applying some pressure, however—with guys who were serious fisting bottoms, who liked the idea as much as I did—I could feel my vertebrae protesting, and I don't need back problems. Some things really are best left in the realm of fantasy.

Walking around the Castro district, all through last summer, I was goggle-eyed. Suddenly, shaved and shorn heads weren't just a phenomenon of the leather scene; now they signified . . . what? I've spent the past year studying that question. Hard work, too: Hanging out in cafes, lusting over every skinhead who comes in. Lots of them lust right back, which is nice, but it usually doesn't lead to anything. But that's one of the characteristics that defines this new skinhead (not to be confused, thank you, with Aryan Nation and other quasi-Nazis): A refusal to give up on sex, plague or no plague. Not all of these men are HIV positive. Hey, not all of them are even gay. Most of them do have tattoos and rings, which is nice; it gives me an excuse to flirt with them. ("Hey, that's a cool tattoo coming up out of your pants. Would you show me rest of it?") But I'd have to describe all of them as Queer, and they are the embodiment of the new Queer God of the Nineties, the man who is learning (all over again, sort of like our predecessors learned in the Seventies) the endless possibilities of Queer Sexuality and Queer Community. And this is the community I've always wanted.

I'm using the word "Queer" pretty freely, here. Yeah, I like it. I've always felt queer, even back in grade school, and it never bothered me. I reveled in it. I did all sorts of things that would show everyone how different I was. l don't ever recall feeling a desire to "fit in." With those boring folks? Please. So yes, when the word "Queer" first began making the rounds, a few years back, I laughed, and said, Yes, this word describes me. Oh, "Gay" describes me, too; but if asked to choose between the two (and they're certainly not synonymous) I think being Queer is more important to me than being Gay. And shaving my head, I've discovered in the past year, is one of the primo ways of announcing to the world (well, the rather limited world of San Francisco) that I'm queer. My tattoo isn't always visible (who can wear sleeveless shirts in this frigid city?) and not everyone knows my face, and I don't feel like decorating my leather jacket with "Silence = Death" stickers, but the shaved head speaks volumes.

Is this true in other cities around the country? I don't really know. In Los Angeles, there's a much lower percentage of skinheads. They're very devoted to their hairstyles in the southland, and sunburn is a bigger problem, too. I haven't been to the East Coast recently, so I don't know the situation there. This may be just a San Francisco thing. At the height of the trend, this past summer, I figure about every tenth man in the Castro had a smooth scalp. A lot of them, of course, were already balding. I look at those men with envy, knowing that their morning shaving ritual is proportionally simpler than mine. That's one of the other features of shaving that really appeals to me: The re-empowerment of those men. For years, many of them have felt self–conscious about their hair-loss. (You wouldn't believe all the ads for hair-replacement in the local gay papers!) This has always pained and puzzled me. Seeing a healthy and vital man get all paranoid about something that I consider a perfectly normal (and extremely masculine) characteristic strikes me as the height of absurdity. Now, with the possibility of "passing" as intentional skinheads, many of these men are regaining their self-confidence, and it's inspiring. Not to mention very sexy.

So, when I get one of these super-sexy shaved scalps rubbing up against me, and I describe what we're doing as "sex," what am I really talking about? I mean, barring the fantasy of head-fucking, there's not a lot you can really do with a head, right? Well . . . I dunno. I've found, over the past couple of years, that there's more to sex than fucking. (And a good thing, too!) When I see one of those shiny domes, I get all funny inside—maybe something like a cat feels when it smells catnip. My nostrils flare, I start to drool and crawl after him . . . well, okay, no, I usually do manage to restrain myself. But I think my most intense urge is just to . . . rub his head. You can attribute this to my obsession with words: The brain, to me, is the primary sex organ. Yeah, sure, I love sucking dick (and ass, and pits, and toes, and lots of other body parts), but a man's head is where it all comes from. And when he shaves it, he's exposing himself to the world in a way that's more intimate, to me, than exposing his dick. He's saying, "These are my thoughts and fantasies, right out there in the open; come taste them." And I do. I rub his head, I lick it, I massage it and caress it and make love to it. I think my intensity communicates itself to most of these guys. They wouldn't be skinheads if they didn't have at least an inkling of how personal a passion they're arousing. When you fall in love with a guy's dick (and I do, now and then) you're separating it from the rest of his body, ignoring the rest of the person. When you fall in love with his head—well, yeah, a nicely muscular body is pleasant to look at and rub up against, but it's the head that turns me on, because it *is* the person.

I don't, of course, limit myself to the freshly shaved. There are equal pleasures to be had from one-day-old sandpaper stubble, and a week-long scrub brush, and even a month's fuzzy growth. Any of these, rubbed against a sensitive tit, or an asshole, is pure sex. Rubbing scalps together, while it can often be more funny than sexy, is still an extremely intimate act that says: We are the same tribe: The Queer Tribe. And if orgasm is really important to him, I'm very fond of kneeling down in front of him and saying, "Please, sir—shoot on my head." Feeling him lick his cum off my sensitive skin comes pretty close to an orgasmic experience. Just so he doesn't take my "Please, sir" too seriously. I can only keep up the act for so long without breaking up.

That, oddly enough, may be the most clearly distinguishing characteristic of the Queer Skinhead, the thing that most obviously sets him apart from the Leatherman, whom he superficially resembles: Playfulness. The ones I've met, anyhow. Maybe that's just another word for rebellion, but these are men who aren't afraid to laugh and be silly during sex, who know that sex isn't quite so serious a business as we were taught, growing up. And that is the one characteristic I'm most fond of in my partners.

An Acquired Taste

I have Jon King to thank for my obsession with sushi. There aren't a lot of foods that I feel truly passionate about, but raw fish is one of them. Predictably, it's one of America's favorite villains: even if it doesn't actually poison you (and to date, in all the hundreds of times I've eaten it, I have yet to be poisoned), most people in this country view it with distaste. Which probably has a lot to do with my devotion to it. I do so love being in the minority.

There was a time when I wouldn't eat fish at all, raw or cooked. When I was a child, I was quite passionate about live fish, and kept a large collection of them in my room. At some point, the mental imagery of eating my pets' relatives got to be too much for my psyche, and I began suffering from a very real psychosomatic stomach distress every time my mom cooked fish. I'd refuse to eat dinner on those nights. You'll notice that I got over it.

Somehow, despite having lived in San Francisco for nearly five years at that point, I don't think I'd ever had sushi until I met Jon King. Not that I was opposed to the idea, but I'm easily intimidated by strange surroundings, and a sushi bar is about as strange as you can get. You're supposed to know what you want. Okay, maybe they aren't actually laughing at those dumb Americans who have to look at the pictures and point to order each dish, but that's the feeling I get whenever I'm on foreign soil. It offends my sensibilities to be unable to order knowledgeably. Okay, I'll be more honest: It wounds my ego. No one's ever accused me of a lack of self-esteem, but cut me, even just a little, and I do bleed.

So anyway . . . sushi bars intimidated me. Jon didn't ask if I'd ever been to one, he just said, c'mon, let's go to lunch—and took me to a place up in Japantown. And that lunch, notwithstanding all of our subsequent encounters (and all the wonderful scenes he committed to video), is the image that I associate most with Jon. This sushi bar—I don't know if it's still there, I haven't been back—was unique among the places I've been in the intervening ten years. The preparation area was an island in the center of the room; the counter ran all the way around. On the counter was a canal, with little barges floating on it. Each barge had a plate of sushi on it. As they floated by, you picked up the plate. When you were finished, the waitress tallied up your bill by the number (and color) of your plates. Ingenious—and more to the point, it took all the intimidation out of the experience, and made it fun. I didn't have to ask for anything by name. I could pick up anything that looked interesting, and try it. Didn't have to display my ignorance. And no, I still didn't know the names of anything, but I knew that I liked it all, and it was worth humiliating myself every now and then for a taste of it.

Now, about that "acquired taste" bit. I'm sure there are such things; I could even name a few that I've acquired. I know that the first time I tasted beer, I couldn't understand why anyone would want to drink it. Foul stuff. It never became one of my favorite beverages, but with time I did learn to tolerate it, simply because it came with the territory: when you're hanging out at the Eagle or the Ramrod, you don't order orange juice. And that was the kind of bar I frequented, back in the days when I could still stand bars. Now that I've given up beer altogether, I can't say that I miss it . . . but I do occasionally remember the way it felt, sliding down my throat, and feel a twinge of nostalgia. More for the associations that go with it—like piss-parties—than for the taste.

Which brings us to that much-maligned subject: taste. I don't think I've ever tried to be an arbiter of taste in gay society; essentially, I don't believe in it. That is to say, in one universal standard by which all others should be judged. Ayn Rand certainly believed in such a standard, but then, Ayn could often be a bit too dogmatic for her own good. No, I believe in tastes, plural, and I think that this is a good thing. My own tastes are culled from many different sources—eclectic, we like to say, rather than random—and I am generally pretty self-confident. If I dress oddly, or furnish my apartment with bizarre cast-off furniture and homemade shelves, with plants growing everywhere and an endless blizzard of papers on my desk—well, the bottom line is, I don't much care what anyone else thinks. I'm living my life the way that seems most comfortable to me, and anyone who fails to understand that is obviously, well, "a man of no importance."

I will confess, however, that there are several items in my wardrobe which I have never been able to force myself to wear in public (but which I likewise can't force myself to throw away, because someday I might feel the urge). The West Point cadet's uniform, for instance, or the red satin pants. I don't think I would regard either of these items as being truly "tasteful," yet both are beautiful, and both require a lot more self-confidence than I have, even when I'm at my best.

But to get back to my unagi . . . well, I've gotten a lot better. I don't have sushi nearly as often as I'd like to: it's one of those things that I reserve for days when I want to be especially good to myself. The doctors, you know, disapprove. Doctors are like that. They think that life was meant to be lived without risks. Now, I don't jump out of planes for fun, and I don't ride roller coasters, and I don't drive my car at excessive speeds. The risks I take, like the other pleasures that fill my life, tend to be of the quiet kind. Sex, for me, is not a "safe" activity; neither is sushi. Trying to make either of them safe misses the point. Do I draw lines based on risk? Not often. For instance, there's that celebrated pufferfish, the one with the deadly toxin in its liver. I don't think it's legal to serve it in the United States (our government loves to legislate the fun out of life), but if I were to encounter it at a sushi bar overseas, sometime . . . would I eat it? I wonder. To begin with, I think it's out of my price range, but I might be tempted. Just to see what all the fuss is about. You can't live your life in fear of what might happen. On the other hand . . . well, I doubt that it would be worth it, taste-wise. A simple plate of sashimi would probably satisfy me just as well.

The question, I think, is: how hard should you try to "acquire" a taste? The whole concept seems to originate in a standardized notion of what we're supposed to like and dislike. I have, alas, an uneducated palate: I don't especially care for caviar, and I wouldn't know a truffle if it bit me. (Chocolate truffles, on the other hand, require no introduction—and no effort to acquire the taste, either.) After due consideration, I have to regard this as a blessing. I can get as much pleasure out of a veggie burrito down at the neighborhood taqueria as I do from a $60 dinner at Oritalia. Sushi generally falls somewhere between those two extremes, price-wise. But my taste buds think it's as close to heaven as they're ever liable to get. And I didn't have to teach them a damn thing.

Learning to Love the Bomb

For the past twenty years, my life has revolved around sex. During my teenage years, I thought about it continuously because I wasn't getting it (or at least, not enough to keep me satisfied). In my early twenties, I stumbled into the world of pornography and became, quite unintentionally, an icon to thousands of horny viewers. AIDS, like it or not, changed the way I looked at sex. For a number of years, my activities were curtailed, but my fantasies and sexual curiosities grew ever more intense. When I retired from the screen and moved to the printed page, it seemed only natural that my subject should be sex. I've been writing about it, some would say obsessively, for the past seven years. I'll tell you right up front that I don't have The Answers. I don't expect to find them, either. I've had a good time along the way, though, and I think I'm gaining a little bit of insight into what makes me tick.

To those people who say I'm obsessive, and darkly imply that I'm an addict who should be in counseling: No, I'm afraid I can't agree. Yes, I clearly have spent much more time on sex, these twenty years, than it deserves. I wouldn't have had to do so, however, if society gave it its proper place and importance. I may be overcompensating, but someone had to, and I elected myself. My audiences seemed to think I did a pretty good job. My goal is quite simple: To make people think about sex. Not just look for it, though I've no objection to that, but think about it. Because it's a subject that deserves thought, and yet we're all brought up to believe that it just "comes naturally," and doesn't need any thought. Bullshit.

Given all this background, many people find it ironic—some of them undoubtedly take a certain vengeful glee in the fact—that a few years ago, my own personal sexual abilities began to wane. This first became apparent in 1988, when the use of condoms became problematic. Let's face it, stopping to put on a condom is distracting, and suddenly, my hard-ons weren't so rock hard that they could stand up to the delay. Oh, I continued to have sex—there are more ways to get off than just fucking—but I was feeling increasingly uncomfortable about my (lack of) potency. I had, after all, a reputation to uphold. Many, if not most, of my sex partners had seen me on video; they had expectations. The gay male community is mostly based on/revolves around sex. I don't think this is categorically a bad thing, but it did mean that when my sexual appetite began to wane, I no longer had as much desire to immerse myself in that community. I began to feel . . . old.

In 1990, for a number of reasons, I fled to a rural retreat where I wouldn't have to deal with sex. For the next two years, my only sexual encounters came on my infrequent trips back to San Francisco, Chicago, or New York. Life was good. Then I met a man and asked him to move in with me—a request that I now count as the worst mistake I've ever made. For three years, my life gradually deteriorated—and my potency along with it. In the past two years, I've managed to get a good solid hard-on about ten times, and it hardly seems worth trying. The pleasure, I'm sorry to say, has gone out of it. Last week, I met a man who was determined to get me to fuck him; he wouldn't take no for an answer. So I gave it a shot. Would've made a great comedy video—me pinching my dick at the base to try to get some semblance of stiffness, then shoving it into him like putting stuffing into a turkey. If I hadn't really wanted to do whatever I could to satisfy him, I would've just called the whole thing off. Well, he did eventually shoot his load, and I was able to sigh with relief and cuddle with him for a few moments. That was a lot more satisfying, for me, than trying to fuck him.

As you might expect, I've devoted a lot of thought, these past three years, to this subject. Trying to figure out what caused it, learning new ways of having sex that get around it, getting over my insecurities and hangups around it. As cautioned above, I don't have Answers. I've got a lot of theories, and a lot of experience, and one bit of news that may surprise you.

Theories. Oi vey. The most obvious "cause" has to be AIDS. Either fear of getting it, or (after getting it) fear of passing it on. And then, of course, as the disease progresses, most PWAs report a "loss of desire" that keeps them from going out looking for sex. Well, yes, I've certainly experienced that loss of desire in recent times, but initially, the desire was just as strong as ever. It was the flesh that was weak. And as for the fear of passing it on to others . . . well, yeah, there was that. Then, in 1992, I discovered the joys of Positive Sex, having sex with other positives, and since then most of my partners (with the notable exception of the aforementioned cohabitor) have been positive. I found that I could relax a lot more that way—and being relaxed, I find, is crucial to good sex.

Playing with Positives. That's come to be an important part of my sex life. Intermingled with this, inextricably, is the expansion of "sex" beyond genital-oriented things like fucking and sucking. I'm not alone in my lack of response to physical stimuli, nor am I alone in my continued need for emotional reassurance that yes, I am still a worthwhile human being, that yes, I am still a gay man, that yes, I am still capable of giving and getting pleasure. I can get these things from other Positives much more easily than from Negatives—from men who have shared the experience of "bed death." Men in the traditional gay community don't want to consider these issues; they don't want to admit that they exist. When I tell a Positive guy that I'm tired, all I really want to do is sleep, and that no matter what he does, I won't be getting a hard-on, he understands (usually). Negatives seldom do; they're usually freaked out by the notion that you can enjoy sex without a hard-on. It's a new concept for them.

There's one other specific physical factor that figures in, here. In May of 1993, I developed a lymphoma around the base of my spine; it cut off a number of nerves, and while it was eventually declared in remission, for most of a year I was essentially unable to feel anything below the waist. Many times during that period, my indefatigable partner tried to excite me. I found his stimulation more painful than pleasurable. Kind of like the sensations you feel when a sleeping limb is waking up. He persisted, however (I do not have a good record of knowing how or when to say "No"), and once actually managed to bring me to orgasm, which was excruciatingly painful.

Sensation gradually returned to my lower half. I began getting hard-ons again, though not with anything like the frequency that I'd been accustomed to previously. And I don't think the nerves in my dick have ever really gone back to "normal." Seems to me that I remember jerking off being lots more pleasurable, once upon a time.

Nerve damage; low energy/low hormone levels; difficulty in communication with potential partners; fear of infection—all perfectly valid hypotheses for why my dick doesn't get hard anymore. I'm sure they all played some part, but I'm inclined to give more of the credit to the psychological part of the puzzle.

When I was a pornstar, I was known primarily for my big dick. Yeah, there were a couple of films in which I got fucked, but mostly, directors hired me to be a top. I was usually expected to demonstrate my prowess at sucking my own dick, too, since that's one of my leitmotifs. Although I was, and always had been, more of a bottom by nature, I laughed good-naturedly and put up with this typecasting, because I wanted to be in the movies. And I was always able to raise a respectable hard-on; it wasn't as though fucking these guys was unpleasant, it just didn't turn me on in the same way that being fucked would have. But I had the title of The Biggest Dick in San Francisco, and directors (and audiences) wanted to see it in action. I performed.

And I came, in time, to resent it. My dick, that is. I didn't much like the way it got all the attention. Anytime I met someone, and he connected me with that infamous title, I knew immediately that he wasn't someone I wanted to spend a lot of time with. I suppose it really is expecting too much, when you've made your reputation as a Big Dick, to expect people to value you for your mind. It seems churlish, I know, to resent the source of my fame and fortune. But I did.

And then, somewhere along the line, my dick stopped getting hard, so I couldn't play that top role anymore. H'mmm. Do you suppose . . . ?

Moving right along to The Worst Mistake I Ever Made. . . . When I asked Larry to move in with me, he announced he wanted a committed, monogamous relationship. I wasn't altogether thrilled with the idea, but I was besotted; I agreed. The romance was fading, four months later, when the lymphoma hit. The question became suddenly moot: I was in too much pain to go out hunting. But it didn't take long after recovery for me to tell him, Uh-uh, no more monogamy for this boy. His persistent attentions during that period had already brought me to brink of physical violence numerous times: I just wanted to be left alone, and he kept trying to rub himself off against me, kind of like a poorly trained dog humping the guests' legs. I began going out and looking for sex, any sex, with the specific intent of reminding myself that yes, sex can still be pleasurable and mutual. Did I find sex? You betcha. Unfortunately, that state of mind—desperation—is not conducive to pleasure and mutuality. Most of what I found, during that period, was rather cold and impersonal sex, better described as "taking out my frustrations." Sex, in other words, had taken on some very unhealthy associations. I recognized it, but I couldn't do anything about it as long as my tormentor was still living with me. Finally, after another year of torture (at which point my hard-ons were almost nonexistent) I vacated the house myself, being unable to oust him.

This sounds uncomfortably like I'm trying to pass the blame. Well, I suppose I am. This man has some of the sickest ideas about sexuality and intimacy that I've ever encountered, and I allowed myself to be subverted by them for the sake of togetherness. Pay attention to those words: *I allowed myself.* I didn't tell him, four months into the relationship, that I'd lost all interest in his body and that I'd really rather he start sleeping somewhere else. Instead, I convinced myself that I could put up with his unwelcome attentions if it meant a stable, ongoing relationship. Remember that dictum, from the Victorian era, of what sex was supposed to be like for the woman? "Close your eyes and think of England." That's what I was doing. Is it any wonder that my dick learned to shrivel up?

One of the few really memorable times in the past couple of years, when my dick was as hard as it's ever been, came when I met a couple of guys at a bathhouse. They were lovers; they were both positive; they were highly uninhibited; and they both loved to be fisted, and had all the gear to prove it. Crisco, poppers, dildoes, you name it. I was enchanted, and also extremely turned on. I've always liked playing with lovers. You get to experience the intimacy, without having to deal with the quarrels and bitching. And I was reminded, for the first time in years, of the incidental benefit of being into fisting: You don't have to have a hard-on. In fact, dicks become almost irrelevant. With that knowledge—the knowledge that I could satisfy them both, without ever getting hard—suddenly my own inhibitions were loosed, and I was more intensely turned on than I'd been in years. Three years, to be precise. I spent the next two hours playing musical asses: Hand in one, dick in the other; then the other way around, hand *and* dick in one . . . oh, it was grand. And damn good for my ego, to see that I was still capable of that kind of intense arousal.

In other words, it was the simple fact that my dick was being ignored (more or less) that turned me on, that made me capable of arousal with these guys. Yes, just in case I haven't made it clear enough: I do think that dicks get far too much attention among gay men. Understandable, yes, given the societal taboos on them, but not healthy. I can think of a dozen body parts that are more important to me, starting with the brain.

I played with this couple on several other occasions, and the sex continued to be good, and exciting. My hard-ons were not quite as hard, but I was still having fun. But . . . all things run their course. They broke up. When I played with just one of them, yeah, I was still able to jerk off inside his ass (a very hot fantasy for both of us), but there wasn't the same boiling passion that I'd experienced in the three-way. I'm willing to attribute this, however, to the more advanced state of my "disability."

Now, speaking of that word, let's get on to some more basic issues. Enough already with the attempts to figure out "Why?" My main concern, since losing my potency, has been "How?"—that is, how to live with things as they are, how to get the most pleasure out of the sex life that I still have. Because, make no mistake, I do still have a sex life. It's changed, true, but I have to say, modestly, that I've had some of the best sex of my life in the past two years—all without ever getting the beginnings of a hardon. Most of these episodes, predictably, have been with men who wanted to fuck me: Men who weren't the least bit disturbed by my limp dick, and in some cases didn't even appear to notice it. You really can't imagine how much of a thrill I got out of that simple fact. Did I reach orgasm? No. But there's a curious sensation I often get when I feel a man shooting his load inside me. I don't suppose there's a clinical term for it, I don't think it's a physical sensation, but a lightning bolt of joy goes from my butt to my brain, bypassing my dick completely, and I feel completely contented. It may sound like sour grapes to many of you, but . . . I think this sensation, whatever it is (and I think it's purely psychological, the thrill of being totally possessed, owned, dominated) is far more intense than the "real" orgasms I was having five years ago.

Moving on . . . well, I'm going to get a little sentimental, here, and possibly challenge your definition of "sex." Kissing and holding are extremely important to me. There are times when I really wish I could just spend the night with a guy, holding him and kissing his neck . . . then turning over and being held by him . . . feeling his breathing all without ever dealing with the more physical, energetic, orgasm-oriented side of sex. I've done this a few times, in the past few months, and one of those nights ranks among my Top Ten sexual encounters of all time. We never even touched each others' genitalia (we both wore underwear), but I felt more warmed and cared for and comforted than I ever did in that infamous relationship. Did I get a hard-on? I don't think so. Who knows, maybe I did in my sleep. Most men probably wouldn't be willing to call that sex; most men probably would look down on it as something suitable for us limp-dicked wussies who can't do any better. Mmmm . . . I may be a Pollyanna (well, I know I am), but it's occurred to me in recent months that I wouldn't have been able to have that experience five years ago. We would have gotten into bed, and whammo! my dick would've been hard, and we'd have been fucking. (This man, I should add, fulfilled every possible criterion for my definition of the word "hot.") I'm sure the sex would have been good. But . . . could it possibly have been as special as this night spent cuddling and kissing? I doubt it.

Again, check out that phrase: I wouldn't have been *able* to have that experience then. In a strange way, it seems to me that I was experiencing a different form of impotence then, more of an emotional impotence. Oh, sure, I had many very intimate relationships, but I don't think I knew how to relate to someone in an intimate way without fucking. This is a lesson that I needed to learn, and apparently I wasn't learning it fast enough, so I was given a little help. Perhaps it seems strange to you, hearing me refer to a limp dick as "help"—but that's me, Pollyanna Pervert.

And while we're on the subject of Perversion . . . well, despite my reputation as an anything-goes kind of guy, I've mostly been surprisingly vanilla in my sex life. Yeah, sure, I can fist (and I enjoy it), but I don't seek it out. And I'm conversant with most of the other varieties of kink: Bondage, S/M, watersports, and leather have all played small but important roles in my life. But over the past couple of years . . . yes, that interest has been revived. You see, you don't need a hard-on to enjoy getting (or giving) a mouthful of piss. You don't need a hard-on to be mummified (though lots of guys do get one). You don't need a hard-on to be intoxicated by the smell of a leather hood covering your nose, or the feeling of being gently flogged. These are what I would call mental exercises in sex: Ways of broadening your response, giving yourself more possibilities, rejoining the sexual community. More sour grapes? If you like. I know that when I'm kneeling in the bathtub at the local sexclub, being pissed on by three guys at once, I feel as turned on as I ever felt with my dick up some guy's ass—even though the news may never reach my groin.

I'm going to insert, here, one more exceptional experience. This happened in November, 1997, on my last trip to New York. I was introduced to a man who wanted to shoot some pics of me—just for his own personal enjoyment. I was happy to agree—shyness not being one of my notable characteristics—with the caveat that I was unlikely to get hard. "That's okay," he said. "This is just for fun." Bingo! He'd said the magic word. Fun. And it was, and we did, and my dick ended up responding as it hadn't in years. I was onstage again, with a rapt audience, and I was suddenly turned on. It helped that he had a room lined with mirrors, and a jar of Albolene (the Official Lube of the San Francisco Jacks), but what was most significant, I think, was the fact that he was using a digital camera. In other words, no "wasted" shots. He could shoot all day and it wouldn't cost him a penny . . . and I'd know, all the while, that he was snapping away because he loved doing it, because he was turned on by what I was doing. No pressure, and lots of positive feedback.

It also didn't hurt that he got more visibly and audibly turned on while shooting than any other cameraman I've ever worked with. He even took a break, halfway through, to show me how good his mouth could feel on my dick. Some people would undoubtedly react to this scenario with outraged charges of "exploitation." Sorry, I didn't notice, I was too busy having fun.

The gay male community, as I stated at the beginning, has been traditionally all about sex. I don't see this as altogether detrimental; it's better than ignoring it, anyway. The problem is that so many gay men have such a limited notion of what that means, and are therefore prone to extreme mental anguish when things don't go according to the script. What I've been learning over the past few years is primarily the importance of keeping an open mind, and taking my pleasure where I find it. You'd think this would be something every gay man would've learned in Coming Out 101, wouldn't you? And maybe we would have, if there had been such a class in high school. But no, each of us has to learn it for ourselves—usually, the hard way, at an age when we've begun to be intolerant of "learning new tricks." AIDS, in that sense, has had a curiously ameliorative effect on many men's psyches: We've been forced to reevaluate lots of the assumptions by which we formerly lived our lives. No small favor, that.

What it comes down to, I think, is the simple statement: sex is mental. This is not news. Most of us, however, tend to forget it. It *seems* like such a purely physical act. We even compare it to animal instinct, denying that it has a psychological component. Big mistake. If you're only paying attention to the sensations coming from your dick, you're missing out on the most intense part of sex. The mind is where it all happens, guys. Notwithstanding any physical nerve damage caused by my lymphoma, I think it was my mind that took away my hard-ons, and it's very clearly my mind that has given me something just as rewarding in return. Imagination, invention, intimacy. No, I don't know how to reverse the process, but neither am I trying. I've been spending some time on that question lately: If I could go back to the sexuality I had, say, ten years ago—or even fifteen—would I? I hesitate to give a definitive answer, but . . . I don't think so. I've learned to love what I've got.

No, Really, I Mean It

Bear with me for a little while. I'm going to confront you with a premise that you may find a bit hard to take, coming from me. Please don't run screaming in horror. It's simple: Sex is unimportant.

Really. Trivial, unnecessary, frivolous, and boring. All of the above. It's been given much too much prominence in our culture, both positively and negatively; I would like to see it assume its proper place in the cultural hierarchy, somewhere between fly-fishing and trash collection. (No, get your minds out of the gutter. Neither of those is a type of sex, dammit!) Basically, I wish people wouldn't get so darned excited about it. It's just sex.

Thus speaks someone who's had just about all he wants, for a number of years, and has now elected a life of near celibacy instead. I probably could still go out to a sex club and have five men in one night; I'm not so old and decrepit that men would flee in horror. But frankly, I'm bored by the idea. And I don't see what the fuss is about. So gay men have a lot of sex, especially in their twenties. Big fucking deal. The various arguments I've heard to promote monogamy—largely based on premises of unwanted pregnancy and absent fathers—don't exactly apply to us. As for diseases . . . well, there are some pretty well-documented ways of avoiding AIDS (and other diseases) without cutting into your sex life significantly. (And on the other hand, as someone who's picked up just about every sexually transmissible disease known to man, I have to say that they're not all bad, either. Worse things have happened to me than getting AIDS, and I lived through them.) Personally, I think promiscuity is nothing more than the sign of a healthy mind in a healthy body.

Which is not to say that all sex is healthy, and that we should all run out and have as much as we can. Looking back at my life, despite all the fun I had, I would have to say that most of the sex I participated in during my twenties was done for the wrong reasons.

There were lots of men who I agreed to fuck just because they wanted so badly to be fucked, without feeling much of anything, good or bad, about them or the act. This kind of depresses me. Yes, I was more than a little bit desperate to be liked. And hey, I generally had a good time—but the best parts of the sex, I've come to realize, came afterward, when maybe he'd talk to me, maybe we'd go out to dinner, or maybe we'd just sleep together. I'm not blaming these guys, mind you; I put on a good show of loving what I was doing, and in truth it was never unpleasant. Just . . . boring. Friction between two mucous membranes. Yawn. Climax. Oh, good, now can we get down to the good stuff?

Okay, I'm exaggerating for effect. It never seemed like this at the time; I always thought I was doing it because it was fun. Why do I have the temerity to reinterpret these experiences now, in hindsight? Just because my life has changed is no reason to try changing history. No . . . but I think I was still operating under the general misapprehension then, to wit, that sex is the most important thing in the universe. If it weren't, why would my parents have been so uptight and paranoid about it? Must be something really special to get all these adults so wound-up . . . etc. So when I went out on my own, I determined (no, not as a conscious statement of purpose, but just as a general mode of life) that I was going to find out everything I possibly could learn about sex. And I did a pretty good job, too. Most of those men, whether or not they entertained me, did teach me a thing or two, for which I'm grateful. Knowledge is never a bad thing, and I'm glad to have studied the subject. But my ultimate assessment is still that it's not as important a subject as most people would like to think.

So why do I keep blathering on about it? Well . . . primarily, because the first step in cutting sex down to size is demystifying it. As a subject, it still has most of the world terrified, like this omnipotent hand of god hovering over their heads. No, folks, it doesn't have to be that way. Sex can be your friend, if you open yourself up to it. It won't kill you. (It's possible that a virus might—but please don't confuse that virus with sex.) And at that point, once we get past this mind-numbing fear, sex will assume its proper role in life . . . and I strongly suspect that gay men, freed of the onus laid on them for centuries by their repressed heterosexual brethren, will heave a sigh of relief and stop wearing themselves out with endlessly repetitive sexual calisthenics. Because that's been part of the myth, too, along with the specter of sex as a tool of the devil: The associated notion that gay men were necessarily *nothing but* sex. And we lived up to the legend, cooperatively—hey, we sighed, it's a lousy job, but someone's gotta do it. It'll be a relief when we can get back to being people, instead of paradigms.

So why has it taken me so long to "come out" about being tired of sex as a subject? This isn't something that came to me on a flash of lightning three years ago; it's a slowly dawning realization, and I've been quite uncertain of whether it was something I wanted to admit. After all, I said to myself, I do have a reputation to uphold . . . and I realized, right there, that I wasn't serious. My "reputation," such as it is, is something I would gladly see tarnished, even vaporized completely. I've made intimations, in articles I've written previously, that I don't feel much like a sex-god. But my fans all seem to go, "oh, pshaw, you're just modest," and adore me all the more. Okay, fine, guys, I don't have any great objection to being adored, but let's do it for the right reasons, okay? A big dick and the ability to fuck are not sufficient qualifications for sainthood, much less deification. I'd like to think that my writing is a little more important to the world than my videos were.

That's the point at which Michelangelo Signorile came out with his latest book, *Life Outside.* He and I had made a virtual art of being on opposite sides of every issue, and I was all set to denounce his latest as another antisex manifesto . . . but when I went to listen to him read, I realized that he was putting down on paper—and putting out there for thousands to read—lots of the same thoughts that I'd been thinking, but hiding. That gay men have been shoved into a mold, consisting of sex, drugs, party life, and perfect pecs, and it was time we broke the mold, and decided for ourselves what we wanted to be. That, after all, was what "gay liberation" was supposed to be about, yes? Being true to yourself, and all those other nice slogans? That's what I thought, when I first came out . . . but then I swallowed the party line (and hook, and sinker) and made myself over into a sex machine. No, not completely; I didn't lose myself in drugs and parties as a lot of people do. There was always "another side" to me that didn't have much of anything to do with sex—but I preferred to keep him hidden away, because, well, he wasn't quite what people expected of a sex star.

And I realized that Mike had done pretty much the same thing, but had finally come out and admitted that he'd been wrong. Wish I'd been able to do that sooner.

Over the past three years, I've had less sex than at any comparable period since I was fifteen. I'm not sure whether to call it "loss of interest or just recognition of lack of interest." The interest may never have been there to begin with; I may have been operating on cultural expectations rather than lust all those years. It's difficult, as I've said before, to interpret the past. But yes, there is a local sex club that I used to go to, once a month or so; I went there regularly throughout 1996. It's a friendly sort of place, where you can go and hang out in the living room and chat with the new arrivals, or nosh in the kitchen (there's always bowls of veggies and chips and cookies for munching), and a wonderful hot tub in the backyard. Not your typical sex club; this is more like a regular brunch crowd. I would go and soak in the tub for an hour, and then wander through the play area. There were always people playing, quite openly, without self-consciousness, and seldom were there crowds of voyeurs, as many people might assume. Sometimes I would play with someone, but usually not. The hot tub, and the conversation, was what I went there for.

Then, in January of this year, I met someone there who quite changed my life. He went home with me, even though I'd told him that I wasn't up for anything sexual, and we talked most of the night. And repeated the exercise, again and again . . . I think it was our third date, or maybe the fourth, when we finally had sex. Was the sex good? Who's to say? I was in love, and there is no objective scale on which to rank such things. We were communicating more intimately than I'd ever communicated with anybody, and what made it all the more remarkable was the fact that I was violently resisting the idea, all the way. For the first month, I refused to acknowledge any of it. "We're having an affair," I said to myself. "I'm not looking for a relationship." Lord knows I wasn't; I was still feeling seriously burned from my last one. But that's what happened.

But back to sex. (Who, me? Distracted?) Oh, sure, we've had sex. At least eight or ten times . . . in ten months. Not quite the fiery passion you'd expect from an ex-pornstar and his brand new boyfriend, what? Fact is, I'm just not interested. We talk, we sleep together, we share more secrets than I've ever felt comfortable sharing with anyone. These are the things of which a relationship is made . . . not sex. (I don't think I'm breaking any headline-making news here, am I?) He's had sex with probably about a hundred other men in these ten months (he's a very vigorous twenty-four, and I wouldn't dream of curbing his sexual appetite; besides which, he does it for a living), and I've had sex with . . . five others. I sucked off two men through a gloryhole at the Unicorn in Chicago in June, which proved remarkably unsatisfying and depressing; spent a wonderful, warm and intimate night with an old acquaintance in Minneapolis, being fucked senseless; and another night at the local sex club last week, which accounted for two more. There was a time in my past when this wouldn't have added up to one remarkable weekend. And yet . . . somehow, I'm happier and more satisfied now than I can ever remember being when I was rushing off to a different bathhouse every night.

Do I expect that this affair, or this lack of libido, will last forever? Please, be serious. Nothing lasts forever. No, sex is not the enemy. Sex is wonderful, and there is no reason to either hide it or hide from it. But by the same token . . . well, I've never been a big fan of obsession. I like my life to be placid and rational, thank you very much, and obsessions tend to be just the opposite. But if there's one thing worse than obsession, it's the pretense of obsession, and I fear that's what I, and many other gay men, have been lured into. It hasn't really hurt us; after all, we know it's just a game. (Don't we?) But really, it's all right now: we can drop the masks, come out of hiding. Be ourselves. Be sexual, yes, by all means, as publicly and blatantly sexual as we feel like . . . but not because it's what's expected of us. That's all I'm saying.

There now, that wasn't so difficult to swallow, was it?

More Reasons Why
I Don't Want a Lover

There are about a million reasons why I don't want a Lover, mostly having to do with the lessons I've learned from past entanglements. Now, don't get me wrong: the relationship I'm in now is the most wonderfully rewarding one of my life, and I'm happier than I've ever been. I don't know how I've been so lucky. But the things that are making me so happy about this relationship are the ways in which it is different from my past mistakes, and different from the societal expectations of what a Lover "should" be. In other words: whatever Chris and I are, we're not Lovers. We've occasionally flirted with using the word, but neither of us really likes to use it. We're not married, we're not monogamous, we're not "a couple" in any of the usual ways, and we're certainly not planning on moving in together. We're two independent people who happen to like spending most of our free time together; two people who get most of our serious emotional feedback and support from each other. It's not about guilt or permanence—which makes it a significant departure from "the norm" in gay society.

In my past relationships, sex was always "an issue." The way in which this issue usually surfaced was in my lack of interest in it: I have never managed to sustain a sexual interest in anyone for more than a couple of months. Familiarity breeds, if not contempt, at least boredom, and while I may have remained in love, my lack of arousal caused such emotional wounds in my partners that I experienced "sympathetic trauma"—and the relationship would spiral downwards into a black hole of guilt and noncommunication. Some would call my loss of interest abnormal; frankly, my dear, I don't give a damn whether it's abnormal or not, it's inherent in my psychological makeup, and I'm tired of feeling guilty about it. And for the first time in my life, I've encountered a man who understands, and doesn't feel rejected; someone who is self-confident enough to accept the fact that there is someone in the world—someone who loves him very much, even—who is not sexually aroused by him. Why should this be such a difficult concept to grasp? Never mind, I don't need to know the answer. I've got a man, now, who's got it.

Part of the sense of rejection undoubtedly was connected to my profession. As a sex professional, I think most of my previous Lovers expected me to always be "on-call," expected that my body was in a state of perpetual arousal. It's not, and it never has been. There was a time, however, when I believed the same thing: I was a liberated gay man, I had a big dick, men were always admiring it, therefore I *must* be continuously horny, right? No, the logic doesn't really compute, but I accepted it back when I was seventeen, and didn't have occasion to question it until my early thirties, when it started causing me real problems. Anyway, this is one of the presumptions in many (if not most) gay relationships (and straight ones, too, I believe): That you should always be available for sex, whenever your partner is feeling horny, because this is what being in love is all about. Do people really believe this shit? I don't know; I know that my last Lover certainly did, or at least behaved like it. He made me feel like a blow-up doll . . . and predictably, as I came to hate him, I came to hate sex. His kind of sex, at any rate: The roll on, get off, roll off kind. And this, I have a feeling, is what a lot of relationships degenerate into. Like it or not, it's there, it's predictable, and safe (from an emotional standpoint), and requires no thought or effort, so you might as well stay with it. I stayed in that relationship about two years longer than I should have . . . every minute of which was progressively worse. I still feel like I'm suffering from sex psychosis due to the mental guilt tripping I went through with that man.

But enough about that. Another aspect of Lovers that makes me shudder is the possessiveness that seems to be part and parcel: The ideas that one man ought to be able to fulfill all of my needs, and that my life needs to be an open book to him. Fact is, there are parts of my life that I don't want to share with anyone, not even my current snuggle-bunny, who knows more about me than anyone else has ever known. And this is something that most men can't understand. This idea of "becoming one flesh," the blending of lives until each partner has no distinguishing characteristics—this is one of the sicker aspects of Lovers, and probably the primary reason for my fear and loathing of the institution. I am an individual, thank you very much; human beings are not meant to be part of a hive mind (which is, apparently, the heterosexual model). The concept of privacy is important to me.

Then there is the philosophical angle, quite aside from these pragmatic analyses: The fact that the whole concept of Lovers is a direct descendant of the institution of Marriage. Now, Marriage may or may not be a good experience for some individuals, but the societal expectations of it are definitely a bad idea. First, that everyone should participate; second, that it will solve all problems, make our lives blissful, and eliminate juvenile delinquency; and third, that the promise "till death do us part" is anything but the most rosy-colored fantasy. All quite ludicrous notions, but all have been adopted without alteration into the gay concept of the Good Life. Nearly every gay man I know is looking for a Lover, certain that he'll be happy if only he can settle down. Expectations like this can't lead to anything but disappointment. Of course there are "successful" relationships—examples are constantly being paraded before us, famous gay couples who have "lasted" thirty, forty, fifty years—but I have a sneaking suspicion that a major part of their success consists of the fact that both partners have kept their expectations in check. Come to think of it, that's a useful formula for all areas of life: Lowered expectations generally lead to pleasant surprises. Society's assumption that a happy, lifelong marriage is the norm is a formula for disaster and disappointment.

More? You want more? Okay, I'll give you more. Fact is, I *like* living by myself. I like being able to work at any hour I feel like it, and I like the time it gives me to think. When I'm saddled with a Lover, he's always asking me to tell him what I'm thinking and feeling. How the hell do I have time to *know* how I'm feeling, if I'm always trying to vocalize it? Contrary to popular belief, the brain does not need to be hooked up to the tongue in order to function. I find it's quite the reverse. When I begin to feel depressed (a relatively rare occurrence for me, generally attributable to spending too much time in close proximity to people who seem to think they're entitled to a frontrow seat at my emotional theater), the last thing I want is a Lover asking me, anxiously, "What's wrong? Is it something I said? Can I do anything to make you feel better?" What I want to say, in these situations, is: Go Away. But of course, that wouldn't make me feel better. It would just make me feel guilty, starting a whole new cycle of depression. But if there is one thing that is absolutely essential to my mental stability, it is Time Alone. Companionship is all well and good, but it can also make me crazy, and the whole phenomenon of Lovers seems designed to eliminate all of that Alone Time.

You may feel that I'm being unnecessarily hard on the institution of Lovers. The fact is, the past ten months have been unparalleled bliss, such as I've never experienced before, and it's very nice to know that two people can become romantically intimate without engaging in ritual emotional disembowelment. Kind of restores my faith in my own adaptability, if not in the intelligence of the species as a whole. (I don't foresee the behavior of the rest of the human race changing to emulate my own.) I fully intend to do my best to keep this relationship going for as long as it remains a psychological credit. But I think I've gotten beyond the stage of needing to keep a relationship alive at all costs, regardless of the emotional liability. And that's the sort of tenaciousness implied, to me, by the concreteness of the term "Lover."

Up in Lights

I can't even remember when it was that I first decided that my home was in the theater. By age thirteen, when I signed up for drama class, my father was unsurprised. While I don't remember any specific incident, he was supportive, and interested in what we were doing. But by that time, I'd already been onstage twice, in two different grade school plays—both of which I'd "written" myself. (One, I plagiarized directly from James Thurber; the other, although I wrote the dialogue, was a hoary old chestnut of a farce about mushrooms. The most notable feature of this playlet was the fact that although six of the seven characters were female, all were played *en travestie*. I was informed by an audience member, later, that I was the only one of the boys who realized that when you're wearing a skirt, you should sit with your knees together.) I may not have been aware, in eighth grade, of the full implications of my fascination with theater, but I did know that I liked being onstage.

I was also a shameless brownnoser, and I was the only boy in the drama class who could read lines realistically, without stumbling over the three-syllable words, so I tended to get cast in the leading roles. This changed, of course, when I arrived in high school as a lowly sophomore, back on the bottom rung of the ladder. But the theater crowd was the most glamorous one I could imagine: Dave Renton and Joel Otterman, the two stars of the department, were my idols. Seniors, of course; Joel was actually going to Juilliard, on a scholarship. I'm afraid I pestered him unmercifully, trying to break down his resistance—to no avail. Seduction has never been my strong suit.

Did I just drift, here, from plays to playing, without even noticing? Well, yes. The two were always rather intimately linked in my mind. My drama teacher for the last two years of high school, Mark Weddle, became the subject of a lot of my nighttime fantasies. (I ran into him on the street in San Francisco, about five years later, when

I was doing jack-off shows at Savages. I invited him to come down and see me onstage. I don't believe he ever showed up, however. While I usually try to avoid making presumptions about other people's sexuality, I'm afraid I'd have to conclude that he was hopelessly heterosexual, and quite possibly unaware of my adoration. These things can change, however.) And then there was the play during my senior year—a tacky musical called *So This Is Paris*—when I was consigned to the dressing room (having done my star turn the previous year). Well, okay, that was fine with me. Helping actors to get dressed is, arguably, even more fun than being onstage myself. One of the actors I helped to dress was Jim Blackwell, a thin, shy, blond boy with delectable lips and eyes, and a voice that almost scared you—it was the deepest basso profundo I've ever heard, and hearing it come from someone so insubstantial was . . . well, incongruous. He was also a friend of mine, and his parents were friends of my parents; we had things in common. He was also rigidly religious, and very conservative. The fact that the role of a Parisian roué required him to wear his shirt unbuttoned embarrassed the hell out of him. The fact that Mr. Weddle wanted him to have chest hair (which I got to draw on him every night) delighted the hell out of me. And then, halfway through the run, Jim and I had that little talk. It's not as if it was any secret around school: I'd been telling anyone who asked for the past year, and word does get around. But Jim was a bit naive. When he asked, and I said, "Yeah, I'm gay," he was more than a bit shocked. And he asked Mr. Weddle to get someone else to do his makeup after that. C'est la vie.

After this . . . well, there was a community college production of *Bells Are Ringing*—I was in the chorus—and then it was off to bigger and better things. College, and men. Don't ask me why I didn't even bother looking for the theater department at UD; I'm not even sure they had one. But over the summer I'd been distracted by sex, and schoolwork was no longer my top priority. Nor was theater. I still enjoyed going to see shows, but for the next ten years or so, my roles were limited to being an enthusiastic (but critical) audience member.

One of the things that began to concern me, as time went on, was the danger of becoming *too* critical. I mean, I saw a *lot* of plays during those years. Much of it was small, fringe-type theater, in the garages and warehouses in south-of-Market San Francisco; occasionally I'd go to see the big-budget shows at A.C.T., but they didn't thrill me nearly as much. And it bothered me that I might be losing my sense of wonder. I mean, there comes a point, if you're seeing two shows a week, when you're tempted to start evaluating shows as either "good" or "bad"—instead of my preferred method, which is to say that I either enjoyed it or I didn't. I think the people who make a living off of critiquing theater—or any other subject, for that matter—inevitably lose their sense of wonder, the ability to simply be entertained. I didn't want to be a theater critic— not if it meant becoming jaded.

There have been many memorable experiences over the years: The "marathon weeks" at the Oregon Shakespeare Festival, where I'd see ten shows in five days, and leave with iambic pentameter buzzing in my brain; *The AIDS Show* at Theatre Rhino, one of the first attempts (and a rather successful one, at that) to find humor in the epidemic; a performance of *Blue Is for Boys* in New York, which I caught between my jack-off shows (7 and 10) at the Show Palace; *Platypus Reveals All,* a revue-style show based on real headlines from the tabloid press; opening nights of *Jerker* in L.A. and *Chess* in London, and closing night of *Passion,* in New York; George Coates' *Right Mind,* which I saw at the Geary Theatre on October 16, 1989, the final performance before the earthquake closed both the show and the theater; and an odd show called *Clip-Krieg: Ein Musiktheater,* which I saw while staying at the youth hostel in Frankfurt. (Afterward, one of the members of the company came up to me to ask if I'd enjoyed it; I had to admit to him, "Ich nicht spreche Deutsch." He looked at me rather oddly, then found a cast member who spoke better English. It was explained to me, just in case I'd missed the rather heavy-handed symbolism (which I'd done my best to ignore), that this was a version of one of the gospels, and the actors were all really missionaries. Oh, geez. And I'd enjoyed it so much, too, before I'd realized what they were singing about. Never mind; the music was still good. I bought the cassette. They clearly thought I was loony.

Oh yes: The poster for the show, which is what lured me in, was a silhouette of a very buff, very naked man, against an interesting

geometric background. I'll admit, I was expecting something a little
. . . different.

All of this time, I kept on hold my childhood dreams of being
onstage myself. Okay, I was jerking off onstage twice nightly, and
this did satisfy the urge, to a large extent, but I didn't have lines.
Considering my difficulty in projection, this probably was a good
thing . . . but it left me feeling vaguely unfulfilled. I was always
emphatic, whenever anyone referred to me as an "actor" in porn
films: I said, this isn't acting, this is performing. Like seals. (A line
from *Fame* always kept running through my head, the professor's
comment about synthesizers: "That isn't music, Martelli—that's
masturbation.") I did, once, audition for a role in a Theatre Rhino
production of *Jerker.* This was when I was in the process of escap-
ing the City, and the chance of appearing in that play was the only
thing that could have held me back. I didn't get it; I left.

And promptly ran into an actor, in the wilds of Wisconsin. Somehow, though I'd been a theater junkie for years, I'd never been
seriously romantically involved with anyone who was really in the
theater. Stephen was. He was Shakespearean to the core. He loved
character roles, and he loved researching them to within an inch of
their lives. I acquired a healthy respect for the amount of work that
a serious actor can put into his work. No, it's not just a case of "get
up on stage and ham it up." Maybe Stephen deliberately made it
look more difficult and arcane than it needed to be; regardless, he
did a good job. And I started to feel envious. I wanted to get back up
in lights. . . .

In 1995 I started writing my own play. After seeing Ronnie
Larsen's *Scenes from My Love Life* in December—and then seeing
Love! Valour! Compassion! in New York in April—I realized that
I'd been selling myself short. You see, for years I'd declined to
write plays, regardless of my fascination with the medium, because,
I explained, I couldn't write dialogue. Suddenly, this rationalization
was taken away. These two plays (not to mention *Angels in America)* had made it to the tops of their respective markets without any
semblance of believable dialogue. So . . . I started writing, and it
was easy. I can fulminate as effectively as Tony Kushner. Fun, too.
So I spent most of the next eighteen months finishing it and polishing it . . . somewhere along the line, it turned into a musical, which

was rather unexpected, but fun. After all, musicals were always my favorite type of music; I just didn't think that for my first show, I should be tackling the rather frightening prospect of lyric-writing. After the first four or five songs, however, I decided I liked it. (We'll let the audiences decide whether or not I'm any good at it.)

That's where I am now: *Ex-Lovers* is being produced by Theatre Rhino this season, and rehearsals start in about a month. I'm not directing, thank heavens. I don't think I like the idea of a playwright directing his own work. (It can lead to some real power trips and persecution complexes.) I'm already planning my next play, and looking for possible other productions of this one. And I feel like I've come home. Now, I'm not putting down pornography, or books, or magazines, or any of the other pursuits I've engaged in over the years. I've enjoyed them all, and I'll probably continue to do so. But theater is where it's at, for me. I think this can be put down mostly to its ephemeral nature: Every performance is magical, because you know it will never happen quite like this again. (And sometimes, that's a good thing. I can recall my share of disasters.) Books are about permanence, or at least our effort to immortalize ourselves. A play may or may not be immortal, but the players assuredly are not. I love the awareness, as an audience member, of the dual nature of any performance: Onstage and backstage. Playwrights love to write about the fun-house mirror of backstage drama; *Kiss Me Kate* and *Noises Off* are the examples that spring to mind immediately. There are others.

My name has been "up in lights" on a marquee twice now. The first time it happened, my first week at the Show Palace, I was thrilled out of my gourd; I immediately snapped a photo of it. The second time was for *Making Porn* at Theatre Rhino, and I took a photo of that one, too. I grant you, it's an addiction. I'd sell my grandmother, if I had one, for another starring role. I think I've recognized, however, that my role is writing. I've had my moments in the light—a good deal more than fifteen minutes, if I do say so myself—and it's time to fade into the wings with the other writers. It's not a glamorous profession, mostly; even Jackie Collins, bless her heart, will never have the universal recognition that Joan has. (And no, really, I am *not* looking to emulate Jackie!) But the idea of sitting in the dark, watching the curtain go up on my very own play (okay, the metaphorical curtain, since Rhino doesn't have such a thing) . . . well, it's enough to take my breath away.

I spoke, last month, to two of my brothers, David and Donald, for the first time in five years. I've always had a fairly cordial relationship with both of them, if disconnected. But when I told them of the upcoming production of the play, the reaction from both of them was the same. "That's nice. Here, would you like to see some more photos of the kids?" It was the first time in a very long time that I'd interacted with anyone so far outside the theater world; someone to whom plays are simply inconsequential. Both of them said something like, "Gee, I can't remember the last time I went to a play." And they are the true offspring of my parents. I found myself wondering, afterward: How did I do it? How did I spring from the same source as these guys? And I'm afraid I don't have an answer. But I'm at least as happy in my world, without children, as they are in theirs. And there's something else I didn't tell them, but which anyone who knows a playwright should take for granted: They're going to end up onstage one of these days, whether they know about it or not.

Handcuffed Together

There's a phenomenon that's been bugging me for a good long time now, in that peripheral-vision way. I was never entirely sure what it was, until it was shoved into the center of my awareness recently. It's the custom of sharing our entertainments. It's almost expected that you always go to the movies, or to the theater, with someone. People think you're slightly odd if you go alone, or they ask you if something happened to your partner. Okay, now admittedly, I've not traditionally been the partnered type, so this was never an issue; my friends knew better than to ask. And it meant that I discovered the joy of going to the theater alone. I learned that I was able to focus much more intently on the play, the plot and the language, if I didn't have someone beside me making his own value judgments, verbally or nonverbally. And pragmatically, I also discovered that a person who shows up at a theater alone *always* gets in, especially if it's getting close to curtain. I usually end up getting the best seat in the house—the seat they were holding for the director, or that major theater critic, or some other VIP. This is what I refer to as "ticket karma." I never bought tickets in advance.

In the past year, all that has changed. I've acquired a boyfriend, one who insists on doing everything together. He feels hurt when I go to see *Pericles* without asking if he wants to go. So, reluctantly, I got in the habit of asking him. "Do you want to go see *Yeomen of the Guard* this weekend?" I'll ask. "Sure," he'll say. Now, is that enthusiasm, or what? This bugged me for a long time, as I say, in a nonspecific way, but I finally realized what it was that made it offensive to me. He was going because I was going. He wasn't going to see the play; he was going to spend time with me. This, to me, is something akin to sacrilege: using a play, even a Gilbert and Sullivan play, in such a cavalier fashion. Fact is, I take my theatre seriously, and *Yeomen* happens to be the G&S show that most intrigues me—and I'd never seen a production of it. I didn't want to go and be constantly aware of my boyfriend sitting next to me. I didn't want the distraction. This sort of thing is appropriate for movies, I guess; after all, movies are endlessly reviewable, you can even get them on video if you're particularly fond of them. Plays are different: You will only see this particular production once. Even if you go back the next night, it will still be a different show. That's the glory of live theater. You've got to pay attention.

So this time (no, this is not the first time this has happened; it's just the first time I've recognized what was going on) I decided not to do it. I told my boyfriend, the night before the show, that I didn't feel like going. "But you can still go," I added. "But I'd rather wait and go with you," he said. Yeah, I know; that's the problem. He didn't care about seeing the play. And he won't see it. I will go next weekend, without telling him—or maybe I will tell him, and tell him why I want to go by myself. If it's an extremely good production, I may wish he'd come with me, but realistically, I know that having him at my side would only have spoiled my enjoyment of it.

There is a popular notion that "Pleasure shared is pleasure doubled." I think this cliché was thought up by repressed Puritans who were afraid of the idea of solitary pleasure, or any pleasure at all for that matter: To them, having company meant that they couldn't get too carried away, that they would maintain a proper sense of decorum. This attitude is epitomized by the comment, usually made with a certain amount of shame, "I got carried away." Getting carried away is a bad thing, according to them, and having someone next to you usually acts as a damper on enthusiasm. Am I stereotyping, here? Possibly. I'm definitely oversimplifying the phenomenon. Still, you've got to admit, the whole idea of having fun by yourself is a very risqué concept in modern life. The ultimate in solitary pleasure—masturbation, an act undertaken specifically for personal pleasure, with no socially redeeming value whatsoever—is still so shocking in American culture that Joycelyn Elders got ridden out of town on a rail for advocating it, and I've even read a recent letter to the editor in a national gay magazine condemning the practice as "an empty and selfish activity." (Yes, the writer hailed from the Midwest.) I expect the letter writer would condemn my own solitary pleasures—eating, writing, walking in the woods, gardening, and theater-going—with equal fervor: Such activities are only socially worthwhile, he seems to be saying, when they are part of a loving and caring relationship and any pleasure is distributed equally between the participants.

Okay, I'm being unnecessarily catty here. There are, of course, times when I want to do things with people, and of course I understand what he's saying. There are few things in life that have as much pleasure potential as relationships. But one of the primary requirements for that potential to be realized—in my opinion, mind you—is the realization that the participants are individuals, with individual and different needs and desires, and not all those desires need to be shared, or even talked about.

My boyfriend gets most of this. The fact that we have most of our sex with other partners is of no concern to him, and my circle of friends, dating back before I met him, threatens him not at all. But what seems to bother him is the notion that I might prefer being alone to being with him. Being alone is, perhaps, too pure an expression of pleasure, i.e., selfishness. Yes, I will freely admit it: I am selfish. My own welfare (of which my happiness is an integral part) is the thing that is most important to me. This is selfishness in its purest form, and I revel in it. In fact, I consider anyone who rejects such selfishness to be . . . well, not entirely in the real world. Taking care of yourself is your first responsibility, and a good measure of how well you're taking care of yourself is how much time you spend alone with yourself. I know there are lots of people who can't stand being alone with themselves, and I quite understand: I don't much like being alone with them, either. And the notion, so popular in heterosexual circles, that your spouse is the person with whom you need to share your whole life, every last friggin' detail of it . . . well, it's largely responsible for my distaste for the institution of marriage. To create another old cliché: If God had meant us to be married, we would have been born with a pair of handcuffs attached to one wrist.

No thank you. I love my boyfriend, and I derive moments of exquisite pleasure from the times we spend together. But I don't think any of that would be possible without the times that I spend alone—and those are precisely the times that make people (including him) worry about me. If I may be permitted one more analogy here: Trying to play a piano duet when neither of you knows how to play the piano doesn't make beautiful music, it merely produces twice as much noise. Me, I'm longing for some peace and quiet.

Love and the Challenger Disaster

After The Wisconsin Experience, I was, shall we say, somewhat dubious about my chances of ever being "successful" in a relationship. I was definitely on the outs with True Love. I continued in that mode for nearly two years, during which I made a number of well-publicized comments about the futility and insanity of monogamy, marriage, and commitment.

Nothing in my outlook changed, but in January of 1997, I met a man who, um, swept me off my feet. For about three months, I was still just as skeptical as ever, but I found myself unable to resist his undeniable charms. This is called being in love. And, I convinced myself, This Time It's Different. It's true, it was different. It was different in two notable ways: First, I think Chris was the first boyfriend I've ever had who was not threatened by my notoriety, my scandalous past, and not intimidated (and/or in lust with) my big dick; and second, we talked more freely and honestly than in any relationship I'd ever had before. I learned that when jealousy is eliminated as a factor, honesty becomes much easier. I learned . . . oh, all sorts of things. And it was undoubtedly the "best" relationship I've ever had, in all aspects: communication, pleasure, sharing . . . I think it was the sharing part that finally did us in.

Yes, as has been made obvious by my use of the past tense, it's over. Why is it that even though I've just declared it to be the best, I was the one to say that it had become intolerable? Largely because of different concepts of what degree of sharing was expected and permissible in an intimate relationship. I've always been a very private person, needing lots of time alone. It's the time when I'm able to write that keeps me sane, and I'm sorry, I couldn't write anything worth reading when Chris was in the apartment, even if he was asleep. I need to be alone for that. This is something that didn't occur to him. He was always around, it seemed. I kept asking him for more space; he kept acting wounded by my rejection of him. Like I say, we had different thresholds of "Acceptable Intimacy."

This extended into areas beyond the sharing of time. Clothes, for instance, and other possessions. Anything that was mine was his to borrow, and vice versa . . . and "borrow," in his lexicon, did not necessarily include the concepts of asking permission and returning the borrowed items. Okay, I'm obsessed by possessions, huh? It made me feel guilty, every time I got angry at him for having taken something of mine without asking, and yet, I did feel angry. This is called taking liberties. And I felt taken advantage of.

Boundaries. That's what this is all about. He didn't have any. And this is at least as much my fault as his because I didn't set any. I could have; if I'd done so much earlier in our relationship, it's possible it might have lasted. But "lasting" is really not the criterion on which I judge relationships. Fiftieth wedding anniversaries appall me. What they indicate more than anything to me is a lack of initiative, a lack of imagination. Stagnation. There were times, with Chris, when I imagined us staying together for the rest of our lives (bearing in mind that the life expectancy of a PWA is rather short, this wasn't a great stretch), and we certainly both treated the relationship as something eternal while we were in it. Perhaps that's the problem with the concept of eternity: No boundaries.

While I was between Larry and Chris, I loudly denounced marriage, gay or otherwise, as the last refuge of the control freak in modern society (now that the feudal system has generally gone out of business). During the past six months (after overcoming my initial reservations, during which period I tended to keep it a secret that I was "involved") I did my best to let everyone and his brother know about my change of heart. This is called "disclosure." See other essays in this volume for various takes on the joys of married life. I tried to emphasize, however, that there had been no basic change, because my position, as always, was, "People Change." That's why marriage (this promise of "till death do us part," and so on) is insane: Pledging that you will never change is the most antihuman thing I can imagine. Change is the very essence of being human. During the past year, my feelings about love changed, for the better. The facts, and my perception of them, remained the same.

Reality didn't change, but being in love allows you to ignore reality. For a while.

And now I'm in shell-shocked bachelorhood again . . . and where does that leave me? Well, the fact that the past nine months were the most deliriously happy period of my life (with the usual rocky spots, naturally) leaves me with nothing but fond feelings. I'm very grateful to Chris for those months of joy, and for the things I learned from this relationship. Nine months of bliss is not to be sneezed at; it's more than a lot of people ever get. I'm not going to go into a vicious antimarriage tirade again. For those who want to risk it, I say good luck. (You'll need it.) I will probably fall again myself— well, the evidence would certainly point that way. I would hope that I'll be able to keep in mind the lessons from Chris—which have very little to do with Chris, I should add, and everything to do with me and my tolerance levels. And next time . . .

Oh, I don't want to make any promises about what I'll do differently next time. Fact is, next time I'll be in love again, and if there's one thing I definitely know from experience, it's that when I'm in love, I do things that I normally would consider totally unacceptable. (Did I mention that Chris is a smoker? And I vow, today, that there will be no more smokers in my life—and I wryly admit that, if I fall in love with one, all the vows in the world will make no difference.) Love is an irrational state. I am normally a rational person, and from that perspective, love appalls me. I'm not the first person to make this comparison, but . . . having spent some time around addicts over the past six months, I'm struck by how similar their drug-using behaviors are to my actions whenever I'm in love. They will talk (the ones in recovery, that is) incessantly about all the terrible things their addiction made them do . . . and then, regular as clockwork, they'll go out and do it all over again. (Some more often than others.) And here I am, doing my best to analyze, while I'm "clean and sober," my love addiction, in hopes that I can control it better the next time. But, as any recovery-type person can tell you, there is no controlling an addiction. It controls you.

Still, I don't think I'm ready for a Love Addicts meeting. Painful though love may be, it's still the source of my most intensely joyful moments, and I don't want to give those up. I saw Chris again today, very briefly. There is no doubt that I'm still in love with him, and probably he with me; just seeing him was painful. But I got through it, and I'll get through this phase, too. I went out to a sex club last night, for the first time since shortly after I met him, and had sex with two men—one a new acquaintance, the other an old fuck-buddy—and felt the warmth of being back in a group of men who I understood. Mark said to me, after I'd finished sucking him off, "I'm glad I have a husband who tolerates my extracurricular playing." I said, fervently, "I'm glad you have a husband, too. Because if you didn't, I'd probably be first in line, the way I'm feeling right now, and I don't need that." What I needed, at that moment, was what he'd just given me: a throat-battering face-fuck, and some warm, caring hugs. And the knowledge that I was going to be able to go home alone, and spend another hour writing before going to bed.

Postscript: This particular breakup lasted exactly three days, and was merely a preview of the final closing night, which arrived two months later, with much less melodrama. I'm very glad, however, that I wrote the above during those three days, and I've left it unaltered.

Unlimited Sex Only $19.95
(Plus Shipping and Handling)

"What is Sex?" asked my boyfriend—and washed his hands. It's a question that has puzzled me quite a lot in recent years, since my more-or-less complete loss of interest in sex-as-we-know-it. Because, you see, I don't feel like I'm getting any less pleasure out of life than when I was getting laid nightly; quite the reverse. I now look back on those nights of bathhouse haunting as an interesting, but ultimately unsatisfying, form of "gay kindergarten." I'm glad I did it; everyone ought to have the experience. I'm also glad I grew out of it. I try not to make judgments about people who continue in that lifestyle. But my definition of sex has changed; it no longer has the same criteria attached to it, and I'm no longer searching for the same ends.

"What is Sex?" I'll define sex for you. It's made up of two unrelated impulses: the need to hold and be held by someone—the need for human contact—and the need to shoot a load. (Women may or may not have this latter need; I decline to speculate.) Some scientists would like to phrase this as "the procreative need." With all due respect, I disagree. I've shot literally thousands of loads in my life, and never once have I expected or hoped that one of my sperms would grow up into a little Scottkins. Most of those loads were shot on my own belly, while lying in my room alone. Although I may well have been fantasizing about someone or something, they really had nothing to do with goal number one, or indeed with anything outside of my own mind and body.

Some of you are going to be disturbed by my callous division of sex into these two camps. Tough shit. That's the way my sexuality is, the way it's always been, and I don't think it's likely to change. I hesitate to make sweeping generalities, but I suspect that this separation applies to most people, whether or not they acknowledge it. You see, in our culture it's an accepted fiction that sex equals love;

that those two impulses should be united, and indistinguishable. And indeed, I've known lots of gay men—men who haven't taken the time to examine these presuppositions, to question the premises on which their personality is based—who don't recognize the difference. They feel guilty when they masturbate, because it's "cold and unfeeling"; or they go out to the baths looking for intimacy. I've certainly made that latter mistake often enough myself. When I'm feeling depressed, it's all too easy to go to the baths, thinking, oh, a little human contact will cheer me up . . . only to find men who aren't interested in anything but getting their rocks off (which is, after all, the traditional function of the baths), which leaves me feeling more depressed than ever. Over the past few years, I've usually managed to catch myself, whenever I'm in danger of indulging in this particular delusion: The baths are a playground, not a therapy session, and misusing them can be dangerous to your mental health. If you're already in a reasonably good mood, they can be a wonderful tonic; if you're feeling lousy, they tend to exacerbate the problem. So the first question I have to ask myself, anytime I'm tempted to go to the baths (or to the park, or the bookstore, or the sex-club) is: What do I want out of this encounter? Human contact, or a belly full of cum?

I'm not saying that sexuality is evenly divided between these two goals, far from it. It varies widely from person to person—and from time to time. There was a time, many years ago, when I had endless opportunity for jerking off, but none for interpersonal contact. Can you guess which one I thought of little value, and which one I wanted more than anything else in the world? When I finally got to hold another man, I cried. Then there came a long period of my life when my primary goal was to shoot as much spunk as I could manage, and while I still jerked off daily (sometimes four, five, or six times a day) it was sex with other men that I was after. It seemed important to me at the time; I joked that I was making up for lost time. (I didn't start until I was fifteen, which I regarded as a waste of several prime years of adolescence.) And hey, some of my fondest memories date from that period—but they mostly have to do with times when I made a genuine connection with someone, rather than the times when I had an especially good orgasm. I learned the truth, eventually, about orgasms: You can do them best yourself.

They're not really a shared activity. I've occasionally been in a situation where I, or my partner, felt the need to cum (or to pretend to cum) to satisfy someone else; frankly, that's indicative of poor communication and bad sex—which may be one of the contributing factors in my two-year inability to get hard with anyone. It's my body's way of sending the message, right off, that I'm not gonna cum, so don't expect it. If that's what you're after, you picked the wrong guy.

I still jerk off, though not anything like as often as I used to do; once a month is about average. My dick doesn't get hard, not in the sense that it used to. It still feels good, though. And none of these changes have diminished my legendary cocksucking abilities, although I generally reserve them for people who I already know and like, sex with strangers having lost most of its allure. Occasionally I even get fucked, if I'm with someone who pushes all my intimacy buttons, because getting fucked is one of those grey areas where the distinction between sex and intimacy becomes meaningless. After all, it's difficult to fuck someone without holding him real close. (They give special classes in how to do this at all the best porn-acting schools.) But sex, for me, has devolved onto "the little things." Talking with Chris; sharing a bowl of strawberries with Bruce on the beach; sitting in the hot tub rubbing Mark's back; dawdling over my morning tea and croissant at Cafe Flore just to drool over the passing parade of devastatingly attractive men— smiling at them, saying hello, and usually getting a smile in return; or just watching my partner—pick a partner, any partner—as he sleeps. These are intimate things, not specifically sexual things . . . and yet, this is the bulk of my sexuality, today. And, for whatever it's worth, I'm happier than I've ever been.

"What is Sex?" Okay, I'll take the plunge and answer that. It's whatever the fuck you want it to be. Different people have different requirements. Some don't think it's sex unless it includes rope; some don't believe it can happen outside of marriage. (Some people don't believe it can happen *inside* marriage, but that's another subject.) The two most common misconceptions about sex are, (a) that it always takes place with two (or more) people, and (b) that it always concludes with an orgasm or two. Silly limitations. Sex is life, and life is unlimited.

Order Your Own Copy of
This Important Book for Your Personal Library!

RARELY PURE AND NEVER SIMPLE
Selected Essays of Scott O'Hara

_____ in hardbound at $39.95 (ISBN: 0-7890-0573-5)

_____ in softbound at $19.95 (ISBN: 1-56023-939-5)

COST OF BOOKS_____

OUTSIDE USA/CANADA/
MEXICO: ADD 20%_____

POSTAGE & HANDLING_____
(US: $3.00 for first book & $1.25
for each additional book)
Outside US: $4.75 for first book
& $1.75 for each additional book)

SUBTOTAL_____

IN CANADA: ADD 7% GST_____

STATE TAX_____
(NY, OH & MN residents, please
add appropriate local sales tax)

FINAL TOTAL_____
(If paying in Canadian funds,
convert using the current
exchange rate. UNESCO
coupons welcome.)

☐ **BILL ME LATER:** ($5 service charge will be added)
(Bill-me option is good on US/Canada/Mexico orders only;
not good to jobbers, wholesalers, or subscription agencies.)

☐ Check here if billing address is different from
shipping address and attach purchase order and
billing address information.

Signature_____

☐ **PAYMENT ENCLOSED: $**_____

☐ **PLEASE CHARGE TO MY CREDIT CARD.**

☐ Visa ☐ MasterCard ☐ AmEx ☐ Discover
☐ Diner's Club

Account #_____

Exp. Date_____

Signature_____

Prices in US dollars and subject to change without notice.

NAME_____

INSTITUTION_____

ADDRESS_____

CITY_____

STATE/ZIP_____

COUNTRY_____ COUNTY (NY residents only)_____

TEL_____ FAX_____

E-MAIL_____

May we use your e-mail address for confirmations and other types of information? ☐ Yes ☐ No

Order From Your Local Bookstore or Directly From
The Haworth Press, Inc.
10 Alice Street, Binghamton, New York 13904-1580 • USA
TELEPHONE: 1-800-HAWORTH (1-800-429-6784) / Outside US/Canada: (607) 722-5857
FAX: 1-800-895-0582 / Outside US/Canada: (607) 772-6362
E-mail: getinfo@haworthpressinc.com
PLEASE PHOTOCOPY THIS FORM FOR YOUR PERSONAL USE.

BOF96